COMPUTE!'s
Guide to
Nintendo®
Games

Steven A. Schwartz

COMPUTE! Books
Radnor, Pennsylvania

Editor: Pam Williams
Cover Design: Anthony Jacobson
Interior Design: Kimberly Potts

Printed in the United States of America

10 9 8 7 6 5 4 3

Library of Congress Cataloging-in-Publication Data
Schwartz, Steven A.
    Compute!'s guide to Nintendo games / Steven A. Schwartz.
       p.   cm.
    ISBN 0–87455–221–4
    1. Computer games.   2. Nintendo Kabushiki Kaisha.   I. Compute!
Publications, inc.   II. Title.   III. Title: Guide to Nintendo games.
IV. Title: Compute's guide to Nintendo games.
    GV1469.15.S37   1989
    794.8'15365 – dc20   89–42903
                                                                    CIP

COMPUTE! Books, Post Office Box 5406, Greensboro, North Carolina 27403, (919)
275-9809, is a Capital Cities/ABC, Inc. company and is not associated with any
manufacturer of personal computers.

Contents

Foreword

The NES Phenomenon

The Nintendo Entertainment System (NES) is currently the hottest-selling game system in the United States. Christmas 1988 sales in the Boston area were incredible; it was a complete sellout. If you bought one, you were in excellent company. Over seven million Nintendo sets were sold in the U.S. in 1988. Toy stores and electronics outlets had the system backordered through the following February.

As hard as it was to find an NES, the situation for game cartridges was much worse. Long waiting lists and lines at the toy stores were common. The most popular games were often spoken for well before they arrived in the stores. It wasn't enough to just have the money. Shoppers had to hunt for a store willing to take it from them.

There are two reasons why this happened. First, Nintendo reportedly had a chip shortage, making it impossible to manufacture as many cartridges as the software publishers and customers wanted. Second, people recognized quality when they saw it. Although the entry-level NES sells for only $100, its games are almost on par with those in video arcades.

The Atari 2600, the first popular home game system, was crude by comparison. The Apple II and other personal computers, although offering many outstanding games, are too expensive for people who just want to play games. By purchasing an NES, however, almost anyone can now afford high-quality games for the home.

What This Book Will Do for You

Since cartridges are expensive—in many cases, exceeding the cost of similar games for the Apple II, IBM PC, and Macintosh—and most NES players are young (between 8 and 15 years old), game purchases are seldom made on impulse. Players carefully decide which games to get next, using a number of different approaches. They swap them with friends, rent them at video stores, and read about them.

Buying the wrong game is a costly mistake. Certainly, times have changed, but $35 to $55 is still a lot of money for a game that may have little play value. This book can help you sort out the winners from the losers.

COMPUTE!'s Guide to Nintendo Games has something for everyone.

If you need help deciding which games to buy or rent, read the reviews and check the ratings in each game's chapter. They'll give you a good idea of which games are for you.

Although adventure and arcade games are still the most sought after and widely played, the book also covers party/adult games, sports, classics, educational cartridges, and games for younger kids. No matter what type of game you're interested in, you can find it here.

If you want to improve your scores, read the "Tips, Tricks, and Strategies" section for each game. You'll find tips of all kinds that will help you get past major obstacles and improve your play.

If you're really stuck in a game, check out the "Super Secrets" chapter. You may find just the help you need!

If you're in the market for a new controller, read the "Controllers" section. Here you'll find in-depth reviews of many of the popular replacement controllers, as well as a Features Comparison Chart that will quickly show you which controllers have the options you want.

If you're a parent and need some help coping with the Nintendo phenomenon, read the "Parent's Guide" at the back of the book.

How the Book Is Organized

Games

To make it easy to find out about the hottest new NES games, the game review chapters are organized alphabetically by game title. There's also a section called "Short Takes" where you'll find abbreviated reviews of several games that arrived too late to be given full treatment. If you're just looking for a game of a particular type and don't have a specific one in mind, there's an index at the back of the book that lists games by classification (arcade, adventure, sports, and so on).

Following the game review chapters is a list of all their Play Value ratings. Although the ratings are subjective and represent my own opinions, the Play Value summary scores give you a simple way to compare games of the same type against each other.

A section called "Super Secrets" follows "Game Reviews." It's packed with special clues and hints for those who have gotten as far they can in a game and are hopelessly stuck.

Controllers

When choosing a replacement controller for the NES, you probably have some specific features in mind. That's why this section begins with a Feature Comparison Chart that gives you the basic information about each controller. The reviews that follow are grouped by manufacturer, rather than controller name. Since several manufacturers make an entire line of controllers—many of which have features in common—it made most sense to present them this way. The section concludes with coverage of several special-purpose controllers that have novel features or unusual designs.

To make the comparison of replacement controllers easy, there's a chart that summarizes their Play Value ratings. This shows, based on each controller's combination of features, construction, and responsiveness, which are best buys.

A Parent's Guide to Nintendo

If you're a parent, you can have more involvement with the NES than just shelling out the cash for games and occasionally playing a few. Here's where you'll find suggestions to help make the NES a learning experience, and for dealing with the violence that's present in so many games.

What Next?

So where do you go from here? Because *COMPUTE!'s Guide to Nintendo Games* was written to meet a number of objectives, what you read will depend on what you need at the moment.

If you're trying to pick out a game for yourself or your child, first decide the type of game you're most interested in, turn to the game classification index, and read the appropriate reviews. You can use the Play Value summary chart to help find the best ones. If you're concerned about violence, check out the ratings in the "Parent's Guide" too.

After you've purchased or rented a game, you can turn to the individual reviews for tips that will quickly help you improve your scores or steer you towards the game's completion.

If you're looking for a new controller, decide what features you want—as well as the ones you can do without—take a glance at the "Feature Comparison" chart to see which controllers meet your requirements, and then read their reviews. You'll also find the "Play Value Comparison Chart" helpful in choosing the best controller and screening out ones that are under-performers.

About the Author

Dr. Steven Schwartz is both a computer and game expert. He holds a Ph.D. in psychology and has written hundreds of articles for popular computer magazines, beginning in 1978 with *inCider* and *Nibble*. In 1983–1985, he was Editor of *Software Digest*, a frequently quoted IBM PC software review publication.

More recently, he was business applications editor for *MACazine*, a contributing editor for *Macintosh Business Review*, and is currently a contributor to *The Macintosh Bible* and *MacWorld*. He has been director of technical services for Funk Software (maker of *Sideways* and *Allways*) since 1985.

Acknowledgments

Several players contributed tips to *COMPUTE!'s Guide to Nintendo Games*. Within the game review chapters, tips are indicated by the initials of the people who gave them.

- Ron Alpert *[RA]*
- Kevin Boyd *[KB]*
- David Bull *[DB]*
- Jim Hadwick *[JH]*
- Bryan McAllister *[BM]*
- Ira Probst *[IP]*
- Joshua Rose *[JR]*
- Evan Schwartz *[ES]*
- Janet Schwartz *[JS]*
- Justin Serulneck *[JuS]*
- Adam Souliere *[AS]*
- Eric Strauss *[ErS]*

Geoff Johnson [GJ], my super play tester, was an enormous help. He tirelessly worked his way through some of the toughest games around, so I could give tips that spanned each entire game. Hope his grades didn't suffer . . .

I'd like to extend special thanks to Tim and Roberta Daly, owners of The Movie Loft in Framingham, Massachusetts, for sponsoring a Nintendo Secrets contest that helped gather tips for this book.

Thanks also go to Alan Turner, Stephen Levy, Pam Williams, and the other hardworking editors at COMPUTE! Books for their continual encouragement and support.

Finally, I owe a debt that I can never repay to my wife, Janet (who swore that Nintendo games were silly *until* I brought home the set), and my youngest son, Evan, (who is the most phenomenal five-year–old game player I've ever seen). Between them, they easily put in as many hours as I did on this book.

Introduction

In presenting the games for the NES, each chapter follows the same format, making it easy to compare one game against another.

Screen Shot

First, there's a representative screen shot. If you're like me, checking out the graphics is a good way to decide if a game is worth having. Usually, if the programmers paid attention to graphic detail, it's a good indication that they put similar effort into designing the game's plot and action.

Game Basics

Next you'll find the basics for each game: *Classification* (type of game), *Players* (1, 2, or 2 simultaneous), *Controller* (the type or types supported), *Pause* (yes or no), *Restart at Last Level* (yes or no), *Manufacturer*, and *Retail Price*.

    Note: Each price listed in this book is the "manufacturer's suggested retail price." Since stores are free to price Nintendo games and controllers as they see fit, prices may vary substantially from one area of the country to another, as well as from one store to another.

    Although there many ways you can categorize games, I used the following five classifications:

    Arcade Games. The emphasis in arcade games is on action. Shooting and running through mazes, for example, are often the focus of these games. (Refer to the "Game Index by Classification" at the end of this book.)

    Adventure Games: Unlike arcade games, adventures usually have a well-defined mission or goal that's reached by solving riddles or mysteries. There is much more to adventure games than just shooting everything that moves. The dividing line between adventure and arcade games is very thin, however. Many games combine elements of each.

Sports Games. This category includes both team sports (hockey, football, baseball) and individual sports (Olympic events, skateboarding, surfing).

Kids' Games. Although many NES games can be played by almost anyone, a few have been written with very young children (ages 4 to 7) in mind. They frequently combine education and entertainment. If entertainment is the game's focus, a kids' game will often have a simplified plot, put less emphasis on eye/hand coordination, and require little more than elementary reading skills.

Miscellaneous Games. This category is a mixture of many game types. It's a "catch-all" category. It can include traditional board games that have been "computerized" for the NES, games based on television shows, and those designed for group play (as at a party). It's clear from the games' designs that many were intended for older teenagers and adults.

Ratings

Each game is rated for several critical components: *Instructions* (quality and clarity of instructions), *Features* (how well the various game elements complement each other), *Graphics* (how the game looks and the smoothness of animation), *Sound* (quality and appropriateness of the music and sound effects), *Challenge* (how hard it is to advance and complete), and *Play Value* (an overall score). Each rating is based on a ten-point scale, where 0 is poor and 10 is excellent.

Play Value is a summary of all the other ratings—an overall score. It makes it easy to compare games of the same type (all baseball or adventure games, for example). Unlike the other ratings, Play Value is calculated from a formula:

Play Value = (.20 * Instructions Rating)
+ (.25 * Features Rating)
+ (.15 * Graphics Rating)
+ (.15 * Sound Rating)
+ (.25 * Challenge Rating)

The higher the weight, the more important the rating is to the Play Value score. Thus, the Features and Challenge ratings, for example, together make up 50 percent of a game's Play Value score.

Sometimes a feature could not be rated (usually Instructions—because the game was a prototype without a manual). In order to allow a Play Value score to be calculated, missing features were scored as the average of all other ratings.

Review

Each review includes a general discussion of the game's theme and plot, and tells how it works. It also points out the game's strengths and weaknesses, and includes detailed comments for each of the rating categories.

Tips, Tricks, and Strategies

Finally, when appropriate for the type of game, you'll find a section called "Tips, Tricks, and Strategies." Here you'll find helpful tips for improving your scores and getting past some of the toughest scenarios and obstacles.

Note: If you're really stuck in a game, glance through "Super Secrets" following "Game Reviews." You may find just the hint you need!

PART I
Game Reviews

1943

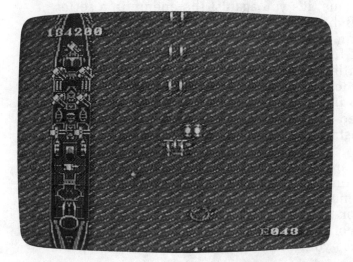

Classification	Arcade
Players	1
Controller	Standard
Pause	Yes
Restart at Last Level	Yes
Manufacturer	Capcom USA, Inc.
Retail Price	$34.95

Ratings

Instructions	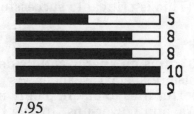	5
Features		8
Graphics		8
Sound		10
Challenge		9
Play Value	7.95	

Review

1943 is an arcade game based on the battles that made up the Battle of Midway in World War II. Piloting your lone P-38 fighter plane, it's you against the enemy in a series of heated dogfights.

The game is divided into missions. In each, you must battle small fighters, bombers, and transport planes that launch additional fighters. In some missions, attacks also come from heavily gunned warships. At the end of each mission is a final fight sequence in which you must destroy a super-sized bomber, warship, or a series of smaller troop carriers. Destroy the enemy and you advance to the next level.

Bullets are your standard weapons. If you shoot a special POW icon, you can obtain more powerful weapons or additional energy. Special weapons and the P-38's energy both work on a timer. When the timer for the former runs out, you revert to bullet fire. When the latter goes, the next hit will cause your plane to explode and end the game.

Instructions

Although an arcade game, the manual is much too skimpy to do it justice. The entire game is described in two sentences, for instance. Although the bonus characters are shown, the instructions don't mention how they affect your score. What's there is relatively clear, but there's simply too much that isn't explained.

Luckily, 1943 isn't tough to figure out. After a few hours of play, you should learn everything necessary and start to work out a strategy for distributing power-up points. (This is critical to successful play.)

Features

The P-38 runs on energy and its destructive power relies on the use of special weapons. As you play, there are ample opportunities to obtain plenty of each by finding bonuses, POWs, and power-ups. To live through the higher-level missions, you may need to find all items of this type. Grabbing them while dodging enemy fire takes a good eye and first-class arcade skills.

4

The bonus characters, however, are unusual for a war game. They include—among other things—a cow, a cat, and a flower. Blow up a ship and a cow appears on its bow. Makes sense to me . . .

Sound and Graphics

The graphics in 1943 are a 50/50 proposition. In the main part of each mission, the water is shown only as a blue pattern with white dots. The enemies are distinct, but there's nothing fancy. It's pretty ordinary stuff. At the end of many missions, however, the enemy is vividly drawn against a brilliant blue background. When it finally explodes, it's very impressive.

The sound effects and music are first-rate. The machine gunfire and explosions are just what a game like this needs.

Challenge

At the lower levels, enemies come down at you from the top of the screen. In the higher levels, there are no such restrictions. Enemies attack from the top, bottom, and sides—all at the same time.

A controller with rapid-fire is highly recommended for playing 1943. Even with it, you'll spend many hours trying to complete certain levels. Without one, your finger will be mighty sore before you get too far.

Play Value

You'll get a lot of play out of 1943. Once a friend thinks he's figured out a mission, just try and get the controller away from him before he's had "one last try."

I'm not sure why, but everyone I know finds 1943 a great game for reducing tension. After coming home from school or work, try shooting down up a few hundred war planes and blowing off steam at the same time.

Tips, Tricks, and Strategies

■ Shoot all the pink planes in each wave. If you miss any, you won't get the chance to power up.

■ Watch for a sparkle of light. When you find one, keep shooting at it to uncover a bonus. Several of the bonuses allow you to add one or more permanent power-up points to your roster.

■ Move the plane away from enemies that are exploding. If you don't you'll lose energy points when they blow.

■ Keep one eye on your energy level (E). If it gets close to 0, any hit taken by the P-38 will end the game.

■ Don't give up too easily. Some missions (like Three) are extremely difficult. Others, even at the higher levels, are a cake walk.

■ To defeat the bomber at the end of Mission Three, try using a combination of lightning and a special weapon.

■ Don't forget about your lightning power (the A button). In the main part of each mission, it will remove some of the enemies. In the last stage of the mission, it will stop the enemy from firing for a short time. Watch your energy, though. Lightning eats it up.

If you've given up on 1943, see "Super Secrets" for more tips.

Adventures of Lolo

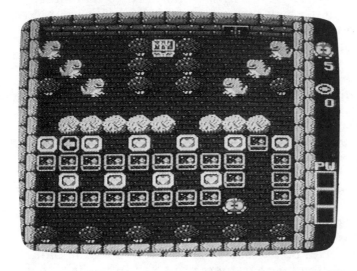

Classification	Arcade
Players	1
Controller	Standard
Pause	No
Restart at Last Level	Yes
Manufacturer	Hal America, Inc.
Retail Price	$38.95

Ratings

Instructions		8
Features		10
Graphics		8
Sound		7
Challenge		9
Play Value	8.6	

Review

Lolo's story line is simple. Princess Lala has been kidnapped by the Great Devil. To save her, Prince Lolo must
enter and make his way through the Great Devil's haunted
castle. Although not especially strong or athletic, Lolo is
very smart. Intelligence (his and yours) is the primary
weapon in the fight for Lala's life and kingdom.

Only the A button and the control pad are used in
Lolo. The button invokes power options and magic shots,
when available. The control pad, as usual, moves Lolo
around the screen. If Lolo becomes hopelessly trapped or
it's obvious that he has made a bad move, you can press
Select to restart the level—with one less Lolo, of course.

Each level is a maze. In addition to the usual assortment of monsters, each maze contains special-purpose
squares called heart framers and emerald framers. Heart
framers occasionally give Lolo magic powers that help him
defend against the monsters or get past obstacles. Neither
type of framer can be crossed or shot through by the monsters. Although the heart framers are fixed in position, emerald framers can be pushed by Lolo to more advantageous
positions, trapping a monster or blocking its shot. When
Lolo has successfully recovered all the heart framers in a
scene, a treasure chest opens. If he can reach the chest in
time, all the monsters will vanish and the door to the next
level will unlock.

If you've successfully done logic problems in cross-
word puzzle magazines, you probably have the necessary
skills to excel at the Adventures of Lolo. Unlike the standard running and jumping games, Lolo is all strategy. Most
levels can only be completed one way . . . go here, grab
this, move the framer here, make the monster follow you
to this spot, and trap him with this. Quick reflexes generally don't help or matter.

Instructions

The instructions are something of a hodgepodge. What's
needed is a simple explanation of the game (clear each
room by removing the heart framers and then get to the
treasure chest before you are caught). The manual is best

used as a reference. Check it as new monsters and environments are encountered.

I like to think of Lolo as an "Oh, yeah . . ." game. Read through by themselves, the instructions make little sense. After playing a few levels, though, you'll probably hear yourself saying "Oh, yeah, *that's* what they meant."

Features

Other than some similarities to the arcade game Pengo, Lolo has several interesting twists. Some of the heart framers are special and give Lolo magic powers, such as the ability to make small bridges appear or to destroy boulders. Others allow him a limited number of magic shots that can turn a monster into an egg or blow it off screen. When in egg form, Lolo can push it into the river and float to a new location.

Any more features than those already included would probably make Lolo too complex to master. Since the buttons are seldom used, this makes it easier to concentrate on playing strategy.

Sound and Graphics

Oh, no! More cartoon music! Luckily, since sound plays such a small part in Lolo, you can turn the volume down or off if it interferes with your concentration.

The graphics are fairly attractive and the characters are easy to recognize. The greatest detail, however, is reserved for the introduction to the game, rather than the game itself. Graphically speaking, Lolo is the most interesting of the lot. He looks like a blue marble with ears and large, expressive eyes. There's also Gol, who bears a striking resemblance to the dinosaurs Bub and Bob (of Bubble Bobble), and a number of monsters who snooze through the game until you awaken them by passing by.

Challenge

Like a chess player, if you can think far enough ahead, you'll make good progress in Lolo. Standard arcade skills— quick turns and a heavy finger on the trigger—will do little for you. There are very few levels you can simply brazen your way through. In general, you have to do it the right way or not at all. Play is simple in the early levels, but, due to the complexity of the mazes, it becomes extremely difficult in the higher levels.

Play Value

Although the characters are cartoon-like and make Lolo look like a kids' game, don't let this fool you. I don't know many young kids who will make it beyond the first few levels. Teenagers and adult players who yearn for a real mental challenge, on the other hand, will *love* Lolo.

My congratulations to the programmers. In a pinch, Lolo could probably serve as part of an IQ test!

Tips, Tricks, and Strategies

- Sometimes being fast is enough. Don't worry about what's chasing you if you can reach the chest before you're caught.
- Rocks and framers block the Medusa's stare. So can other characters if you move or lure them into position.
- Sometimes you can use an Emerald Framer to block *two* squares at once. Sometimes you have to.
- Unlike the Medusa, Gol can only fire in the direction he is facing. Don't be afraid to sneak behind his back.

If you've given up on the Adventures of Lolo, see "Super Secrets" for more tips.

Anticipation

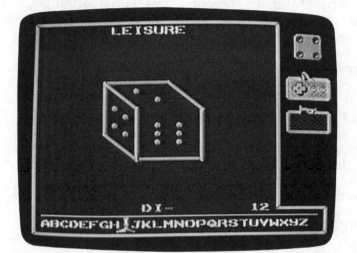

Classification	Miscellaneous (Party)
Players	1 to 4
Controller	Standard
Pause	Yes
Restart at Last Level	Not Applicable
Manufacturer	Nintendo of America, Inc.
Retail Price	$34.95

Ratings

Instructions	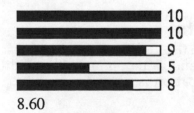	10
Features		10
Graphics		9
Sound		5
Challenge		8
Play Value	8.60	

Review

Anticipation combines elements of the paper-and-pencil games Hangman and Connect-the-Dots with those of the board game Trivial Pursuit. The object of Anticipation is to correctly guess and spell out the name of an object being drawn before your opponent(s) or the NES does. Like Trivial Pursuit, each contestant has a playing piece that's moved around a track. There are squares of four different colors, and each color stands for a different puzzle category. There are 16 puzzle categories, including science, office, music, tools, and "whatchamacallit."

A die counts down from 6 to 1 while the drawing is made. If no one answers in time, a new drawing is started. Otherwise, the player who "buzzes in" first (by pressing a button or the control pad) gets first crack at spelling the name of the object being drawn. If a mistake is made, there's one more chance to do it right. If both answers are wrong, the player has to sit out the puzzle while the other players take a try.

If the puzzle is answered correctly, his playing piece is moved the number of spaces shown on the die. If no one gets it, another puzzle in the same category is drawn.

Once you correctly answer a question for each color, you advance to the next level. There are four levels in the game. In the easiest levels, the line-by-line drawing is done by connecting dots that appear on screen. Spaces for the letters in the answer appear at screen bottom and the puzzle category is also shown. As the difficulty level increases, fewer or no dots at all will be shown, and the category and letter spaces will be omitted.

Instructions

The instructions satisfactorily describe the playing procedures and game options. It isn't difficult to figure out how Anticipation is played.

Features

Anticipation can be played at four different skill levels from easy to very difficult. Up to four players can compete; a maximum of three can be computer players.

In the upper levels, gray squares appear that, when landed on, let the player select the next color category. There are also holes that, when fallen into, drop your playing piece back a level.

In games with three or four human players, the controllers are shared. To buzz in, one player uses the buttons and the other uses the control pad.

Sound and Graphics

The music is the weakest part of Anticipation. Mostly, it's just annoying. Sound effects, as expected, are minimal.

Good graphics are restricted to the boards where the playing pieces are displayed. The pencil draws only thick lines and dots, so it would have been pointless to enhance the graphics in this part of the game.

Challenge

It's tough identifying objects from rough line drawings, particularly at the higher levels where clues aren't given. Children, however, being more shape-oriented, often seem to have an easier time than adults. Being able to spell and having a decent vocabulary helps, though.

The computer players don't intrude too heavily. But when they do, they answer almost immediately—after only a couple of lines have been displayed. Many of their guesses, however, will be wrong.

One thing that adds difficulty to Anticipation is that many objects have a number of different possible names, including slang ones. One that stumped me was a fir tree. I guessed "tree" and "Christmas tree," only to be beaten out by the computer with the answer "Xmas tree."

Play Value

Anticipation is great fun! Everyone I know who has tried it (especially adults) become instant fans. No matter how well written, though, any description of this game will make it sound silly and dull. You'll have to try it before becoming a believer.

Tips, Tricks, and Strategies

■ Watch the die count when you answer. If possible, try to make the next move to a colored square you haven't already dealt with.

■ Be sure to answer before the timer runs out.

■ When you reach level 4, keep track of where the holes are. Make sure that when you answer, the die count isn't on a number that will drop you through a hole. If it will, enter the wrong answer—there's no penalty for doing so.

■ Keep an eye on the screen when a computer player guesses incorrectly. Some correct letters will briefly appear.

Bionic Commando

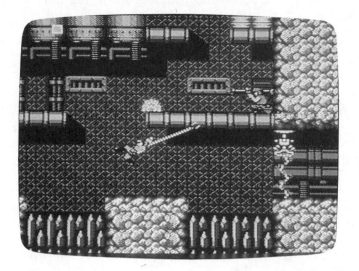

Classification	Arcade
Players	1
Controller	Standard
Pause	Yes
Restart at Last Level	Yes (see text)
Manufacturer	Capcom USA, Inc.
Retail Price	$42.95

Ratings

Instructions		2
Features		9
Graphics		10
Sound		9
Challenge		10
Play Value	8.00	

Review

If war-time action is what you're hankering for, Bionic Commando is one of the best war games around. It's exciting, requires that you master some complex moves, and has stunning graphics.

Outfitted with a rifle, communicator, and a special bionic arm, your task is to move behind enemy lines and rescue Super Joe, the *real* hero of the story. (Yes, it seems kind of silly. *Joe's* the hero. You're just this guy who hangs around and happens to have a ten-foot–long bionic arm.) There are 20 areas you must fight your way through to complete the mission. In most, you'll find plenty of enemies to fight: soldiers with rifles, bazookas, bombs, and laser cannons. In the neutral zones, you'll bump into allies who offer important clues and special weapons.

When choosing an area to transfer into, it's possible to meet an enemy truck. If you do, a special fight sequence begins in which your arm works like a whip. The gun works best for frontal assaults and the arm can be used to ward off bombs.

Instructions

It's too bad that the manual was written by someone with only a passing familiarity with English. Sentences like this abound: "Rocket Gun—It penetrates and destroys, enemies, you can shoot continuously." Even if you can make sense of the manual, you'll still have to spend time discovering the game basics. The instructions fail to mention most of them. (See "Tips, Tricks, and Strategies," below, for a head start). It's a classic example of just how useless game documentation can be.

Features

Bionic Commando has loads of special weapons and interesting fight sequences.

Sound and Graphics

The graphics show a lot of detail and are an excellent example of just what the NES is capable of displaying. The sound effects are equally good. The gunfire, for instance, is surprisingly realistic.

Challenge

You start with three lives. Don't be surprised if you don't make it out of Area 1 in the first several hours of play. Bionic Commando is *not* a piece of cake! It was only after several hours that I discovered there was a Continue option. (If you haven't figured out how this works, see "Super Secrets" for the details.) Knowing it's there should give you some hope.

Play Value

Bionic Commando is an extremely fast-paced game. It has outstanding graphics (the characters look realistic and don't flicker). Unfortunately, it comes with one of the worst manuals around. It seems a shame to have obviously spent so much effort on programming without giving similar attention to the manual. It's still a lot of fun, but you'd better plan on a lot of trial and error before you learn what's going on and what's expected of you.

Tips, Tricks, and Strategies

- If you don't feel like reading a message for the umpteenth time, you can press button B to get past it. Be sure to use your communicator whenever there's an opportunity, however. Read at least part of each message before you press B. If you don't, you may find your progress in the area completely blocked.
- Don't give up simply because you've been knocked off a ledge or a platform. Try grabbing something on your way down. (If you're quick, you can even snag the rocks at the bottom of the cliff in Area 1.)

■ If you're having trouble mastering the bionic arm, it works like this: Up, left, and right motions are made by pressing the control pad in the appropriate direction; diagonal movements are automatically made in the direction you're facing—as long as you don't touch the control pad.

■ The bionic arm is good for more than just reaching and swinging. You can push enemies away with it. If you've killed an enemy, you can also use the arm to grab the bullet that's left behind.

■ When you're asked to select a new location to transfer to, you don't have to go where the game suggests. Use the control pad to pick any area that's adjacent to the one you're currently in.

■ Soldiers that fire from behind barrels always fire in a pattern: stand and shoot, squat and rest. As soon as they stop firing, pull yourself up to a standing position and begin firing. You'll pick them off the moment they rise.

■ Pick up flares in Area 13 before venturing into Area 4. (It's dark in there!)

■ If your Bionic Commando is dying off too quickly, look for a helpful bonus in Area 15.

■ Try ducking when the remote control soldiers come for you. If all else fails, try whacking them away with your arm.

■ There are several types of communicators hidden throughout the game. Search for clues that tell the areas in which each one works.

■ A controller with rapid-fire is a real plus. The sound effects make it sound like a machine gun.

If you've given up on *Bionic Commando*, see "Super Secrets" for more tips.

Blades of Steel

Classification	Sports
Players	1 or 2 simultaneous
Controller	Standard
Pause	Yes
Restart at Last Level	No
Manufacturer	Konami Industry Co. Ltd.
Retail Price	$39.95

Ratings

Instructions	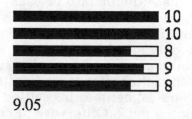	10
Features		10
Graphics		8
Sound		9
Challenge		8
Play Value	9.05	

Review

If it's rock 'em sock 'em hockey action you're looking for, Blades of Steel has it. It's got it all: realistic-looking players, eight teams, faceoffs, checking, penalty calls, fist fights, and Sudden Death overtimes.

In one-player games, you can either play a single Exhibition match (selecting both teams) or compete in a multiple-match Tournament (selecting only your own team). The NES selects all of your opponents. In two-player games, only Exhibition play is available, and each player picks his own team.

Instructions

The instructions are clear and to the point. After reading them, it's merely a matter of practicing your moves and learning to use the controls.

Features

There are three different difficulty levels (junior, college, and pro), eight different teams, and exhibition and tournament play.

Passing the puck is performed by aiming the player who controls it at a teammate and pressing B. Shooting has also been simplified. Where the current shot will go is always indicated by a flashing arrow in the net. When the goalie isn't blocking the shot, just press the A button. All you have to do is watch out for other players who may interfere. The goalie, by the way, can only move left and right, and a little forward or backwards. He's not allowed to leave the net, even to return a shot that's just a few inches out of reach.

The only penalties called are icing (shooting the length of the rink), and slashing or checking. When play gets rough—the latter offense—a fist fight erupts between the two players. Sometimes it's settled quickly with one player grabbing the puck. Otherwise, it continues until one player is knocked down. The loser gets tossed into the penalty box until the referee blows his whistle.

Sound and Graphics

The sound in Blades of Steel is quite good. Several phrases ("Face off!" "It's a pass," and others) were digitized for the game. The music is fun to listen to—what little there is of it. As usual, crowd noises (made mostly of pink noise) are somewhat annoying.

The graphics are a little weak. Since players flash as they're activated, it's sometimes hard to tell who is who when the team colors are similar. On the whole, however, they're good for a game of this sort. It's fun watching the players' little legs pump as they skate.

Challenge

Play against the computer, particularly in the two higher-difficulty levels, is rough. If you want to be humiliated, start with the Pro level. Actually, until you get your moves down, you're better off sticking with the Junior league games or playing against a friend. These play modes offer your best chance to be evenly matched while learning how Blades of Steel works.

Play Value

Blades of Steel is a fairly realistic portrayal of the great sport of hockey, miniaturized for the NES, of course. It's a lot more fun than the old hockey sets we had as kids (the ones where long metal rods skate the players down the ice and spin them around so they can hit a plastic puck). In my case, I also found it more fun than playing hockey itself. You don't get nearly as cold and you get to keep your teeth!

Tips, Tricks, and Strategies

- Keep your goalie lined up with the arrow if you want to avoid a lot of goals. [ErS]
- If you get too close to the NES-controlled goalie or try to take the puck away from him, you'll end up on your face.
- Don't pass blindly—whether you're controlling the goalie or another player. If a teammate isn't visible, you'll usually lose the puck.

■ Don't forget that when you're playing defense, you can switch active men by selecting one with the control pad and pressing B.
■ It's easy to win most fights. Forget about protecting yourself with A button, and concentrate on punching with the B button. (This works best if you have a rapid-fire controller.)
■ If you get tired of looking at the score screen, you can press Start to make it go away.
■ If your team is Minnesota, try some shots from the blue line right after the faceoff. [ErS]

Blaster Master

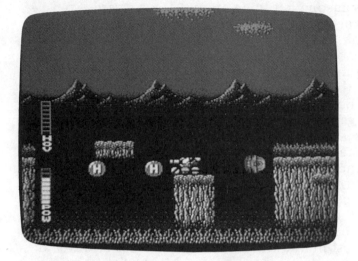

Classification	Arcade
Players	1
Controller	Standard
Pause	Yes
Restart at Last Level	Yes, five times
Manufacturer	Sunsoft
Retail Price	$25.95

Ratings

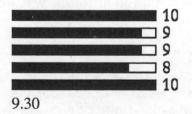

Instructions	10
Features	9
Graphics	9
Sound	8
Challenge	10
Play Value	9.30

Review

Blaster Master is the story of Jason and his frog, Fred. After escaping from his bowl and bumping into a radioactive chest that someone left lying around Jason's yard, Fred becomes a giant mutant. Falling into a hole with Fred, Jason finds himself in a strange radioactive world at the earth's crust that is controlled by mutant bosses (created from nuclear waste materials). It's his mission—and yours—to battle his way through eight difficult stages and destroy the Plutonium Boss in the final stage.

At the game's start, Jason finds an armored vehicle that's just his size, and is suitable for protecting him against the radioactivity and many of the monsters controlled by the Plutonium Boss. Some areas, however, are too small for the vehicle to pass through, so Jason must sometimes explore on foot. In each stage, Jason must find and defeat the mutant boss that controls it. As each boss is beaten, Jason acquires new weapons and special objects that will assist him in his quest. If Jason loses all three of his lives, the game can be Continued (a maximum of five times).

Instructions

Instructions are clearly explained. To help find your way around the world of Blaster Master, the instruction booklet provides a map of stages 1 through 7. A "Special Hints Chart" explains which powers are obtained for defeating each mutant boss, and includes some additional information on moving around in and between stages. More hints on what the different weapons are best for, however, would help.

Features

As in many games of this type, Blaster Master offers its share of special weapons, objects, and powers. To succeed, Jason must constantly be on the lookout for power-up capsules. He can collect power, hover, and gun capsules that will increase his life force, hover ability, and gun firepower, respectively. Special weapons capsules (homing missile, thunder break, and multi-warhead missile) can

24

also be found in some spots. Capsules frequently appear after shooting a mutant or, in the secret room scenes, another object.

As mutant bosses are destroyed, Jason earns valuable weapons, objects, and abilities. These include a super cannon, a door key, and the ability to hover, swim, and climb walls.

Sound and Graphics

The quality of graphics varies within each stage and between stages. In the secret rooms that Jason enters, the detail is very crisp. Outside, however, things tend to be a bit fuzzier. Confrontations with several of the giant mutant bosses are truly awesome and stunning.

The fast-paced theme song helps move the game along, but like so many other game songs, gets boring quickly. The sound effects, mostly gunfire and laser cannon noises, are very good.

Challenge

Living long enough to find the mutant boss in each stage is half the challenge. (If you don't bother with the maps or have trouble reading them, you'll find this extremely challenging.) Because Continues are limited and progress can be very slow at times, completing Blaster Master, since it must be done in one session, is extremely difficult. It's a big game.

Play Value

Defeating the hideous, giant mutants is a lot of fun. Their size and ugliness makes this part of the game considerably more exciting than battling the standard NES mutant. Limited Continues, coupled with the difficulty of progressing between stages, make this a game you won't quickly master.

Tips, Tricks, and Strategies

■ To destroy the multibarreled laser cannons in stage 1, it's safest to shoot from below. They can't fire in a downward direction.

25

- You can get multiple power-ups from some capsules you find. The trick is to take them initially, and then enter a doorway. When you come back out, the capsules will be available again. *[ES]*
- Hyper doubles the attacking power of your gun and all other weapons. *[GJ]*
- The mutant boss for each level is usually as far from the start of the level as possible. If you have to choose between passageways, the longer one or the one furthest from where you started will usually be the right choice. *[GJ]*
- The secret to destroying the mutant frog in Stage 4 is to pay attention to its hops. It uses its tongue after the first three hops, fire droplets after the next two, and the fire missile after the next three. As long as you stay away from the front of the frog when the first two are fired, you won't be hit. When the frog fires the third, run in one direction (not away from or towards it) and it'll miss you. You will only be able to successfully fight back after its first two attacks—by going beside it and striking when its mouth is open. *[GJ]*
- The lobster in Stage 5 is best defeated by staying back and attacking with the two most powerful guns. Using bombs is very difficult and gets harder as time passes. (It blows bubbles that keep you from getting close.) *[GJ]*
- Lava is difficult to get out of. But don't panic. If you wait a second or two before trying to jump out, you won't get stuck. *[GJ]*
- Sometimes it's best to fight enemies from outside your vehicle, particularly if they aren't very powerful. The advantages are that full energy is restored when you re-enter the vehicle and that it will not sustain any damage while you're away. *[GJ]*

■ Be careful where you go. Some areas you can enter have no exit. For instance, there's a spot on the ice level where you must shoot upwards to break blocks and enter a door. When you return, the blocks will have reappeared with no way to break them. *[GJ]*

■ When your character dies, he starts at the last door visited with everything he possessed intact. When you Continue, on the other hand, he starts at the beginning of the level without special powers or weapons. *[GJ]*

If you've given up on Blaster Master, see "Super Secrets" for more tips.

Bubble Bobble

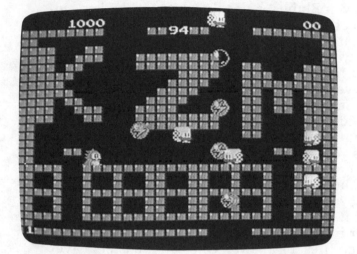

Classification	Arcade
Players	1 or 2 simultaneous
Controller	Standard
Pause	Yes
Restart at Last Level	Yes
Manufacturer	Taito Software, Inc.
Retail Price	$36.99

Ratings

Instructions		8
Features		9
Graphics		7
Sound		8
Challenge		8
Play Value	8.30	

Review

Bubble Bobble is the story of Bub and Bob, two baby
bubble-blowing Brontosaurus buddies. *(Try saying that
fast)*. Baron von Blubba, a deadly white whale, has kidnapped two of Bub and Bob's friends and carried them off
to the evil forest. If they can make it through the Baron's
realm (two worlds with 113 levels each), they just might
rescue their friends.

Each level pits the Bronto buddies against a group of
the Baron's monsters. Each type of monster has its own
characteristics. Some chase, some breathe fire, and some
just flit about hoping to bump into you. Each time an enemy touches you, a life is lost.

The only weapon Bub and Bob possess is the ability to
blow magic bubbles. If they're close enough to an enemy,
they can blow a bubble to trap it. Popping the bubble by
jumping on it, ramming it, or shoving it into a wall causes
the monster inside to change into a bonus object, such as
candy, french fries, or a jewel. Once all monsters have
been defeated, you advance to the next level.

In addition to moving back and forth and making small
hops, Bub and Bob—if they're gentle—can hitch a ride on a
rising bubble. Bubble riding is often the only way to get at
the monsters near the top of the screen, so the technique
must be mastered quickly to progress in the game.

Instructions

The instructions are clearly written and illustrated, but
lack detail. That is, there's enough there to play the game,
but not to excel at it. For instance, "The value of a (Round
Clear) bonus depends upon the color (of the bonus objects)." How? The enemy characters are nicely drawn and
named, but little is said about them.

Features

Bubble Bobble includes many bonus objects. Once in
awhile, a letter in the word EXTEND will float down the
screen. If all the letters are caught, a level is skipped.
Other magic objects allow you to skip up to five levels,
give Bub or Bob magic powers, add an extra life, or help
destroy the monsters on the current screen.

A password option lets you restart (with one or two players) at any level. When your character loses all his lives, you can always restart at the current level.

Allowing two players to play at the same time is a good way to encourage cooperation between kids, particularly since each has to help the other in order to complete many levels. Competition is still present, though. In bonus rounds, 100,000 points go to the winner and 50,000 to the loser.

Sound and Graphics

Cute theme song; it moves the pace of the game along. Music is also effectively used to warn of Baron von Blubba's approach. Bubble Bobble has only a few sound effects, but they work well.

The graphics don't have a lot of flash, but are satisfactory. Characters show flicker, especially when moving at high speed or when many are onscreen at the same time.

Challenge

Most levels can be beaten if you have enough patience. Sometimes it's a matter of waiting for a magic bonus item to either whisk you to another screen or to help destroy the monsters in the current one. Other times, you'll have to use a little strategy. For the very advanced levels, you'll need a lot of strategy, as well as practice, skill, timing, and luck.

Play Value

Bubble Bobble is easily one of the cutest games for the NES. The tail-wagging dinosaur buddies are adorable. Violence is virtually nonexistent. This combination makes it an excellent first game for young kids. Unfortunately, bubble riding is hard to master and takes practice. Playing with a more skilled player on the second controller will help kids advance to higher levels.

Adults, too, seem to get a kick out of Bubble Bobble. The difficulty of making it past the final screen of the first 113, however, can be extremely frustrating.

Tips, Tricks, and Strategies

■ Learn to ride bubbles as soon as you can. Some levels can't be completed until you do. One common mistake is to think that you have to keep pressing the A button to keep bouncing up. In fact, once you're on a bubble, just hold the button down. You'll bounce smoothly to the top.

■ Try to cluster several bubble-encased monsters together before you pop them. The more you pop at one time, the more points you'll receive.

■ If there's no obvious way to get at the monsters above you, try blowing bubbles in different directions or from different places. Sooner or later, you'll usually find a spot and direction that makes them rise.

■ In level 22, use the thunder bubbles to take out the Hullaballoons.

■ If you're stuck on level 30, try this trick. Stand on the legs of the boxes in the middle of the screen. Then bounce up and blow a bubble to trap the creature in the box above. (You can use this trick on a lot of levels.)

■ Ride bubbles to the top of level 38. Then try to pop the fire bubbles so they'll land on the Coileys.

■ Although most of the levels can be beaten with strategy and practice, level 99 is really challenging! After hours of practice, you'll beat it and the challenge screen that follows. But you'll find it's not enough to just beat it; you have to beat it the right way or it doesn't count. You must grab the crystal before it disappears and then perform an additional act (see "Super Secrets").

■ If you complete level B2 with a partner, you must also have a partner to beat the next screen. And you both must live, or it won't count.

If you've given up on Bubble Bobble, see "Super Secrets" for more tips.

Bump 'n' Jump

Classification	Arcade
Players	1
Controller	Standard
Pause	Yes
Restart at Last Level	No
Manufacturer	Vic Tokai Inc.
Retail Price	$34.50

Ratings

Instructions	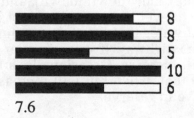	8
Features		8
Graphics		5
Sound		10
Challenge		6
Play Value	7.6	

☐ Bump 'n' Jump

Review

Bump 'n' Jump will remind you of the bumper car ride at the county fair. Your girlfriend has been kidnapped by an evil gang. To rescue her, you'll have to chase the gang in Popper, your souped-up car.

All action takes place on the highway. It's you against the Jackals, the gang that ran off with your girl. To defeat them, you must stop their cars any way you can. By steering correctly, you can sideswipe them and force them into the side of the road, bump them from behind, or brake quickly in front of them. If it's going fast enough, Popper also has the ability to jump into the air. If your timing is good, you can land on the enemy vehicles and crush them.

In addition to the Jackals, other vehicles share the road with you, including trucks, bulldozers, and cement mixers. Periodically each will drop something appropriate onto the highway—sand, oil, or cement—that, if you bump into it, will do some serious damage to Popper. Be careful!

Instructions

The instructions are sparse, but are sufficient to get you going. Better illustrations of the vehicles would have been helpful.

Features

The controls are simple to operate. Even kids should find them easy to master. The A and B buttons are for jumping and braking. The control pad is used to increase Popper's speed (up), slow down (down), and move side to side.

Each level is a long stretch of highway with walls or areas of water that Popper must jump over. Power barrels litter the highway. If you run over them, your energy and fuel will increase. Occasionally, a trucks will drop a 1-UP symbol that, when hit, will increase the number of Poppers you have in reserve.

Sound and Graphics

The music and sound effects are very well done. The graphics, however, offer little to get excited about. All shapes are distinct and easily recognized, but the use of patterns—particularly for some of the backgrounds—leaves much to be desired.

Challenge
With a little practice, most players should be able to get to level 3 consistently. Going beyond that will take a *lot* of practice.

Play Value
Bump'n' Jump should appeal to younger kids. The controls are simple to learn and use. Almost anyone should be able to finish the first level or two. A Continue option would have added to its play value, though. Beginning with the third level, the road gets narrow and treacherous. Since it's hard to get beyond that point, some kids may decide to shelve the game.

Tips, Tricks, and Strategies
- One way to force cars into the side is by jumping in front of them and braking.
- If you're about to run off the road, try jumping. You may be able to avoid the crash.
- Don't linger behind trucks. Too many road hazards are deposited there. Keep your eyes open, though. That's also where you pick up extra cars.
- You can jump on the trucks for big points.
- When a vehicle drops a hazard, there's a warning sound.
- Any time you hear the warning signal or see the flashing "!," get up to speed quickly. You must be traveling at least 150km per hour to jump.
- When you get to the end of a section of road, if you're fast you may be able to push a car or two over the edge before you jump.
- At the end of the first two levels, you can collect a large bonus if you make your buggy jump right into the center of the painted symbol.
- Jump often to get through level 3. There are too many narrow roads where you can be forced off if you just drive.
- There are repair stations hidden in the game. See if you can find them.

35

California Games

Classification	Sports
Players	1 to 8
Controller	Standard
Pause	No
Restart at Last Level	No
Manufacturer	Milton Bradley Company
Retail Price	$40.00

Ratings

Instructions	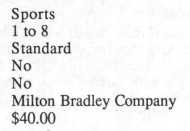	10
Features		9
Graphics		5
Sound		7
Challenge		7
Play Value	7.80	

Review

It's time for fun in the sun with some nontraditional sports. California Games lets you and up to seven friends compete in six events: half pipe skateboarding, foot bag, surfing, roller skating, BMX racing, and Frisbee (flying disk) toss and catch.

You begin the game by entering your name or initials and choosing a sponsor (Milton Bradley, Kowasaki, Maxx-Out, Ocean Pacific, and so on). For each game, you can either practice, compete in some events, or compete in all events. The practice option gives you unlimited practice on any event. Since a failure always starts you over at the beginning, you'll need to spend some time in actual competition if you want to see what the rest of the BMX or skating course looks like. Controller 1 is used by all players and passed among them for each turn.

After each event, scores are reported and trophies are handed out to the winners. At the end of the competition, high scores are recorded.

Instructions

California Games has one of the better instruction manuals around. The moves for each event are clearly described and, when necessary, illustrated. Scoring procedures are also explained. There's even a short glossary of "California" terms included in the back. It's like a totally tubular manual, dude!

Features

California Games includes six events with a variety of stunts you can perform in each. In BMX racing, for example, you can do wheelies, jumps, forward and backward flips, and 360-degree turns. In the foot bag contest, there are 11 different tricks you can do.

Make a mistake in some of the more dangerous events, and something unpleasant will happen to you. In the half pipe, the skateboard hits you in the head. When skating, you fall flat on your face on the pavement.

Sound and Graphics

The music is simple, but pleasant. Lots of California sounds, including the opening lines from "Louie, Louie." There are no sound effects at all, but most of these sports can do without them. The graphics make heavy use of vivid colors, but have a fuzzy quality to them. Everything is discernible, but nothing is distinct.

Challenge

The difficulty of the events varies considerably. Some you'll pick up quickly. Others will require practice along with careful study of the instruction manual. Events such as the half pipe, foot bag, and BMX have many advanced options. To do well, you have to hit the right buttons in combination with the right direction on the control pad at the right moment. Others—surfing, skating, and flying disk—are more a matter of timing and direction than anything else.

 The events that gave me the toughest time were the half pipe skateboarding and BMX racing. If you take advantage of the practice session option, however, you can make consistent progress in almost any event.

Play Value

Becoming an expert in six different events is no small task. Many are simple enough to give good play for even the youngest kids. Others will take more practice and require the ability to pick the right button and control pad presses at the best time. Once the different events are mastered, however, California Games' play value will quickly peak.

Tips, Tricks, and Strategies

- In the half pipe skateboarding contest, hold the control pad down at the start to get up speed. You can follow this with one- or two-hand plants for an easy score.
- To get the speed you need for an aerial turn in skateboarding, you'll have to press up on the control pad as you move up the ramp.

- Surfing moves are made from the surfer's perspective, not yours. If you're not getting anywhere, try holding the controller upside down.
- If you want to be just ahead of the breakwater, do a complete counterclockwise circle as your first move in the surfing contest.
- If you have trouble getting up speed for the initial jump over the grass in the skating contest, go around it (lower edge).
- Don't bump the edges when skating or you'll fall on your face.
- There is a variety of bonus available in the foot bag contest. Try mixing turns (axles) with your tricks to make sure you get the bonus.
- Use a head bounce in the foot bag contest to move your character and the bag off the left-hand side of the screen. You can get as many five-in-a-row scores as you want by continuing to bounce the bag off your head.
- If you want to get a lot of practice under actual contest conditions (picking up where you left off rather than starting over each time), register as all eight contestants.

Castlevania II: Simon's Quest

Classification	Adventure
Players	1
Controller	Standard
Pause	Yes
Restart at Last Level	Yes
Manufacturer	Konami Industry Co. Ltd.
Retail Price	$43.95

Ratings

Instructions	8
Features	10
Graphics	9
Sound	9
Challenge	10
Play Value	9.3

Review

Castlevania II: Simon's Quest is the tale of the return of Dracula. You play the role of Simon Belmont, the hero who originally defeated Dracula. Simon has learned that he now bears Dracula's curse. The only way to remove the curse is to find Dracula's five body parts—they're well hidden within the mansions of Castlevania—and destroy Dracula once and for all.

Along the way, you can enter towns and grill the locals for clues. Monsters of every type imaginable try to halt your progress. As your experience increases, you can purchase more exotic weapons with greater stopping power than your simple leather whip. Magic items, including a few of Dracula's body parts, are great aids to solving Castlevania's many mysteries. It's adventure at its best.

Instructions

The instructions, although complete, could use a few hints. A map, too, would be a big help to most players.

Features

Castlevania II includes the usual assortment of magic items, experience points, and weapons. To buy an item, you must first acquire the requisite number of hearts by defeating monsters and then find someone who will sell the item to you.

Although much of the game is arcade style, to finish it you must find and decipher the game's many clues. To complicate things further, some clues are misleading. Others are outright lies.

In order to map Castlevania, it would have been helpful if sign posts named every new section—village, swamp, forest, cemetery, and mansion. Each village does have a sign that names the areas to its left and right. Unfortunately, there are so many alternate routes that go under or past, it's hard to make a usable map.

Also, although you can enter a password to restore an old game, you always start at the first town, regardless of where you were when you recorded the password. Your last set of weapons and life force will be intact, however.

Sound and Graphics

Castlevania II, thanks to whoever designed the graphics, is stunningly realistic. The music is exciting and adds to the drama. *After playing for more than five hours at a stretch, however, you may want to turn the volume down. Even your favorite album would get boring after five hours.* The only noticeable sound effects are those made by weapons and the fish men leaping from the water. Nice splash, guys.

Challenge

Because you have unlimited Continues and password re-starts, you'll find the challenge of Castlevania II lies not in beating the monsters, but in finding the mansions. My hat is off to anyone who can reach them all without help.

Play Value

Castlevania II is an outstanding example of NES adventure games. It's exciting, the monsters are interesting, and you have to be constantly on the alert for important clues. There's a real feeling of accomplishment when you make it past a point where you've been stumped for several hours (or days).

The game's greatest weakness is that it's easy to get stuck. This is often because you missed picking up an important item, or you've made the right move but in the wrong place, with the wrong item in hand, or for the wrong amount of time. Plan to start over or backtrack several times before you make real progress.

Tips, Tricks, and Strategies

■ Buy holy water immediately. Of all your possessions, this is the most versatile. It can be tossed at monsters, used to uncover hidden objects behind bricks, and thrown at the floor to reveal areas of pavement that aren't as solid as they look. Holy water is unlimited, so use it everywhere.
■ Talk to boarded up windows.
■ Don't believe everything you hear.

- Any room that seems empty may, in fact, hide a secret passageway. Use holy water to reveal it.
- If you're short on power after dark, you can hang around the towns. There are plenty of safe places to stand where nothing can reach you. Killing zombies and vampire bats is a nice way to pass the time and pick up hearts, anyway.
- Some monsters attack by jumping. If you want to stop them easily, make your first move before they have a chance to jump. If possible, use your whip on their ankles.
- Fire stuns monsters and keeps them frozen in their places. But to use it, like many other weapons, you must pay a price—in hearts. *[GJ]*
- When you get the chance, buy a full complement of garlic and laurels. To use them, first move the control pad's cursor into the selection screen panel that contains them. Then continue pressing right or left until one is chosen. After pressing up and the B button to drop one, immediately go back to the selection screen and choose a different object. (It's easy to use them all up by mistake if you don't.)
- If you want to upgrade your crystal, find a helpful prince. There are two of them.
- Two mansions are hidden beneath the water. You'll need to hold a particular object if you want to reach them without drowning. *[GJ]*
- You can swap garlic in the graveyards for special objects. *[GJ]*
- The ferry man knows where to take you by what you're holding. *[GJ]*
- Some staircases are invisible. Try walking up to find them.
- Don't spend time trying to find a town to buy the fire whip in. It can't be bought; it must be bestowed on you. The same goes for the silver and golden daggers, and the silk purse.

■ Some rivers have bouncing stepping stones for you to jump across. The key to moving from one to the next without falling into the river is to jump as each one rises. The closer to the top the stone is, the further you'll jump.
■ Hold Dracula's eyeball to reveal hidden mysteries. *[GJ]*
■ Don't shy away from monsters in the mansions. If you run past them, you may miss a crucial part of the puzzle.
■ Save your passwords at regular intervals—say, after completing each mansion. This makes it easy to backtrack if you need to.

If you've given up on Castlevania II, see "Super Secrets" for more tips.

City Connection

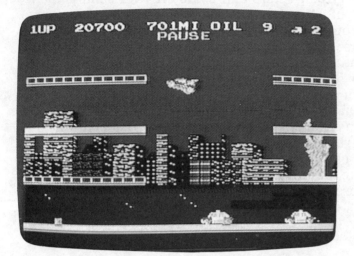

Classification	Arcade
Players	1 or 2
Controller	Standard
Pause	Yes
Restart at Last Level	No
Manufacturer	Jaleco USA, Inc.
Retail Price	$32.99

Ratings

Instructions	████████████████	10
Features	██████████████	8
Graphics	██████████████	8
Sound	████████████████	10
Challenge	██████████████	8
Play Value	8.70	

Review

In City Connection, you're a crook who has broken into a New York City paint store and made off with some expensive paint. Unfortunately, the paint cans are leaking. So as you drive, you cover the highway with paint. To make matters worse, the police are hot on your trail. To elude them, you must lead them on a merry chase through six world cities. To move from one city to the next, you have to cover every inch of roadway with paint.

Other than maneuvering your car out of the way, your only weapons against the police are the oil cans you find on the road. If you press the B button, you toss an oil can at the cops, causing their cars to go into a spin. Bump them while they're spinning and you can knock them off the road. You lose a getaway car for smashing into a police car, hitting a cat, or running into a roadblock.

Instructions

Great instruction booklet; it's very clear.

Features

Given that City Connection is an arcade game, there are a reasonable number of features, including bonus points and warp zones (catch three passing balloons and you jump to a random higher level). I'd like to see a way to continue from the last level, however.

One of the more interesting obstacles is a wayward cartoon cat that plops itself down in the middle of the road. Hit the cat and it flies away—and your car crumples. If dogs had opposable thumbs, City Connection would be their favorite game.

Sound and Graphics

Both music and sound effects are outstanding. All show excellent craftsmanship —from the simple boinking sound of an oil can bouncing off a police car to the tremendous crash as your car blows apart.

48

The graphics are nicely done, particularly the highway scenary. One country's predominantly pink background, though, makes it hard to see the cars, and the police vehicles throughout have a tendency to flicker.

Challenge

For a seemingly simple game, City Connection is tough to master. Until you start watching for balloons, you'll end most games in level 2. Be careful as you explore the higher-level cities. Cars will occasionally travel at you, instead of going the same direction you are.

Play Value

Practice does pay off. At first, I thought I'd never get any further than level 2. After a few days, however, I found that it was easy to get to levels 3 through 5. Easy, that is, once I learned how to catch balloons. City Connection is a fun, if occasionally frustrating, game for all ages.

Tips, Tricks, and Strategies

- The secret to doing well at City Connection lies in learning how to jump. To jump up a level, you must press up and hit A a little in advance of where the jump must take place. To stay on the same level, press A but don't touch the control pad. To go down a level, do nothing. To drop an extra level, press down on the control pad when leaving a level.
- Don't stay on the same level for more than one full trip around. The cat and the pillar will show up quickly if you do.
- If you can't stop in time to avoid the kitty, try to jump over it.
- Since it's tough to notice every balloon that floats by, get a friend to serve as a spotter. Be "balloon conscious." As soon as you grab three of them, you'll warp to a new level.

If you've given up on City Connection, see "Super Secrets" for more tips.

Clash at Demonhead

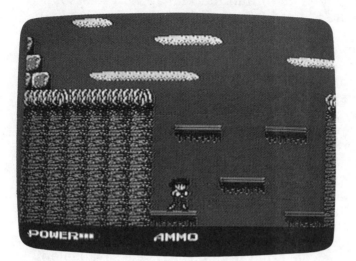

Classification	Adventure
Players	1
Controller	Standard
Pause	Yes
Restart at Last Level	Yes
Manufacturer	Vic Tokai, Inc.
Retail Price	$41.95

Ratings

Instructions	Not available
Features	10
Graphics	10
Sound	9
Challenge	9
Play Value	9.5

Review

As Bang, a top agent for the world security force in year 199x, it's your mission to find the kidnapped Professor Plum before he's forced to construct a doomsday bomb. If you can't find and stop him in time, you'll have to defuse the bomb yourself—making the world a safe place once again. To complete the mission, Bang must find a set of medallions that are very well hidden. And until you find the right clues, they'll stay that way.

Like any good secret agent, Bang has access to a variety of super powers and protection devices. Unfortunately, his agency is cheap, but can coaxed into selling him whatever he needs—if he has the cash. Whenever he has enough money, he can issue a Shop Call to summon the floating weapons store. Whatever items are in stock can be his for a price.

On the mission, Bang can increase his force by obtaining apples, and his life by finding hearts. Money, and gold bars that can be converted to money, are also available if he knows where to look.

Instructions

Not available for review.

Features

Clash at Demonhead has some of the most imaginative critters found in an NES game. My favorite is a sort of flying ball that sticks out its tongue as it hurls energy bombs at Bang. **Obscure reference:** *Many of the characters look like something Robert Crumb might have drawn if he had worked for Walt Disney.*

Sound and Graphics

The sound effects are outstanding. Gunshots and explosions are very realistic. The music, however, isn't quite as catchy as some other games of this type.

The graphics are easily some of the best around. A lot of time must have been taken to design Clash at Demonhead, and it shows.

Challenge

The ability to acquire special weapons and other devices for his arsenal, and the constant need to replenish Bang's force all add greatly to the game's excitement and challenge. These factors, coupled with the need to find clues, let Clash at Demonhead cross the fine line between arcade and adventure game.

Slow and steady progress can be expected with this game. If you stick it out, you'll eventually destroy the monsters that are keeping you from your goal.

Play Value

Clash at Demonhead is constant action and a game of discovery. To win, you must explore every route. Don't be surprised to find yourself backtracking frequently. You'll have to in response to some clues.

Tips, Tricks, and Strategies

- There are secret passages between routes, but to find most of them, you must first complete a special mission or task.
- To get past the fish under Route 6, the most natural thing to do is jump for the bars of gold and then try to shoot at the fish when you fall back into the stream. Unfortunately, it's also the wrong thing to do. Instead, shoot first and then jump. Once you get the timing down, you can pass unscathed through this region.
- You'll meet your first real challenge on Route 11. If you plan to live through it, enter via Route 9 and be sure your energy level is high.
- You can go back and forth on Route 13 for easy money.
- Route 14 is a good place to stock up on hearts and gold.
- Don't forget to visit the sprite on Route 17.
- Rescue the hermit and you'll receive a new power.
- Before doing battle with the demon, go back and forth on Route 33 until Bang is fully charged.
- Go to Route 40 and place the stone over the statue's chest.

- Always keep at least *two* spare Shop Calls. Because of the way they float down, it's possible for one to slip past you. If it's your last one, you'll have to find a free Shop Call hidden in the game.
- Some routes are one-way only.
- Try diving down into any water and lava you find. Be sure you're wearing the proper gear if you don't want to drown or fry.
- Don't rely too heavily on the microrecorder. Although it does save Bang's position and weapons, his force, money, and power drop to default values.

If you've given up on Clash at Demonhead, see "Super Secrets" for more tips. You'll also find the following map a big help in your explorations.

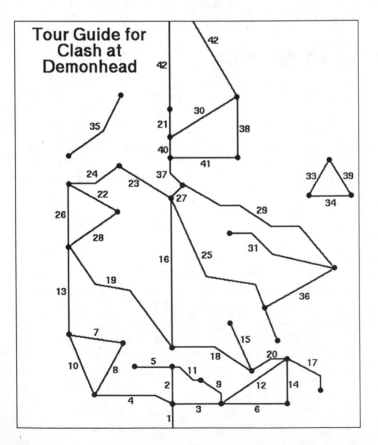

Tour Guide for Clash at Demonhead

Double Dragon

Classification	Arcade
Players	1 or 2
Controller	Standard
Pause	Yes
Restart at Last Level	No
Manufacturer	Tradewest, Inc.
Retail Price	$44.95

Ratings

Instructions		6
Features		9
Graphics		10
Sound		9
Challenge		8
Play Value	8.3	

Review

Double Dragon is about violence, pure and simple. The
game begins with a group of thugs punching your girlfriend
in the stomach and carrying her unconscious body away.
Your task is to defeat everyone who stands in your way in
order to secure her safe return.

Your character (Billy Lee) advances in Double Dragon
by beating up attackers with karate moves and any weapon
he can lay his hands on: knives, baseball bats, whips, and
dynamite. The attackers include blacks, Asians, women,
white street punks, and deformed mutants.

You score points for making successful moves. Each
time you accumulate an additional 1,000 points, you're
awarded an extra "heart." As your hearts increase, you de-
velop new lethal karate and judo moves, including the
hair-pull kick (grab the opponent's hair and knee him in
the face) and the pin attack (jump on the enemy when he's
down and punch him in the face).

Instructions

The manual is the weakest part of Double Dragon. Although it explains how the controls are used to execute
each fighting maneuver, it fails to explain which fighting
techniques are available at each heart level, and what the
screen indicators (life level, hearts, and so on) mean. Players shouldn't have to discover a game's basic features.
That's not adventure; it's sloppiness.

Features

Although generally excellent, there are several "bugs" in
Double Dragon that, if you're not careful, can badly affect
your score. The first is in Mission 1 with the second group
of Lindas. At the scene's right is a place where you can
climb up a wall. If you climb high enough, there's no way
back down. All you can do is wait for the timer to run out.
Another involves the Lindas and a series of ladders. If you
climb one of the ladders too quickly, your character also
disappears. Here, however, you can continue to fight (even
though you can't see what's happening) and your character
will reappear if he wins.

One needed feature is the ability to duck. Slugging it out toe to toe with the giant Abobos is usually a losing proposition. Being able to duck their punches and come back with a move or two would add to the game's realism and play value.

Sound and Graphics

The game features a rousing musical score. Good stuff. The graphics in Double Dragon are also also first rate; a clear 10.

Challenge

With the exception of the giant mutants at the end, it's pretty easy to finish the first three Missions. Getting past that point, however, is another story.

Play Value

Violence aside, Double Dragon is a fun, exciting game to play. Mastering the various moves and figuring out the best way to beat each group of attackers requires strategy and perseverance. It's these qualities that helped make Double Dragon a best seller for Tradewest.

Tips, Tricks, and Strategies

- Many of the fighters are slightly off screen. Don't rush blindly into them. Let them come to you.
- If you're getting hit too often, try holding still. Since all attackers automatically follow your movements, they'll come to you. Start kicking before they arrive and you'll frequently connect without being touched.
- Whenever possible, use your enemies' weapons against them. Using a weapon lessens the chance of getting hit yourself.
- Your life is renewed at the start of each new mission. If you're cagey, you can use this to your advantage.
- In Mission 1, right after defeating the Williams, climb the ladder on the wall. When the Lindas climb up after you, you can kick them off without being touched. This makes it a snap to get the whip.

- You can dodge some types of attacks. When an attacker comes at you with a barrel, crate, dynamite, or a knife, wait until it's thrown and then move quickly up- or down-screen out of the way.
- After defeating the Lindas in front of the elevator shaft in Mission 1, enter the shaft, face left, and start kicking before the action in the next scene starts. If you don't, you'll be trapped between two Lopars and will lose life points unnecessarily.
- The easiest way to beat the Abobo on the conveyor belt is to jump onto the belt as soon as he appears. Since attackers always mimic your moves, he'll follow you onto the belt. Kick him off the end. (Note: *If you do this, you'll lose the opportunity to earn valuable points. If your life force is strong, fight him. If you get close to dying and he's still standing, then kick him off the belt.*)
- The name of the game is hearts. The more hearts you've earned, the more new moves you can make. You may not have noticed, but some attacks are awarded more hit points than others. Point values include whip (30), baseball bat (25), punch (20), kick (15), jump kick (12). To advance quickly, use the high-point attacks as often as possible.
- In Mission 2, you'll have to climb a fence to fight a Williams carrying a baseball bat. Kick him before he can swing, if possible. Also, don't just walk off the end of the wall. Jump if you don't want to lose life points.
- After defeating the Lindas on the construction site, you're expected to climb to the top and fight a lone Chintai. If you have enough life points left, go for it. If you're close to running out, go to the top of the building and when the Chintai comes out, go back down two flights of stairs. You'll move directly to Mission 3 and, as always, your full life points will be restored.
- Here's another trick you can use with the Chintai on the construction site. Jump over him so you're to his left. Then keep kicking him until he falls off the edge of the building.

■ After defeating the attacker on the bridge in Mission 3, jump across. As soon as you land, be ready to move quickly to avoid the knife-wielding Williams on the other side. (Carry the bat along when you jump. It's usable on both sides.)
■ Master the pin attack. It's deadly.

If you've given up on Double Dragon, see "Super Secrets" for more tips.

Golgo 13

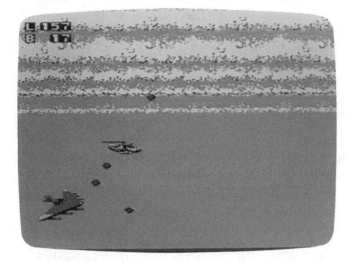

Classification	Adventure
Players	1
Controller	Standard
Pause	Yes
Restart at Last Level	Yes, 52 times
Manufacturer	Vic Tokai Inc.
Retail Price	$38.95

Ratings

Instructions		8
Features		9
Graphics		10
Sound		10
Challenge		8
Play Value	8.85	

Review

Golgo 13 is the game with everything . . . adventure, action, and even a little romance. It also has the most confusing plot of any NES game on the market. Included in the groups involved are the CIA, a secret international organization called FIXER, the KGB, and the remnants of the evil DREK empire. (If you aren't Jewish, the latter won't mean much to you. Think it's a coincidence?)

A CIA helicopter has been shot down over New York City. The helicopter contained a germ warfare weapon called Cassandra-G along with plans for its creation. Both the weapon and plans have mysteriously disappeared from the crash site. Duke Togo, secret agent Golgo 13, has been accused of the shooting, and it is suspected that he is now working as a double agent for the Soviet KGB. The object: Help Duke solve the mystery and clear his name.

As he moves through the different scenes, Duke meets friends as well as enemy agents. Clues that the friendly agents offer help direct Duke's movements throughout the game. If he fails to follow their directions or shows up at meeting points earlier than expected, the agents will stop giving clues or simply turn him away.

Instructions

Most of the necessary game-play info is there. Little, however, is done to help unravel the plot. Maps of several areas are supplied. Telling which one goes with each part of the game, however, is difficult because, although the maps are labelled, the areas in the game don't always have signs that say "You are here."

Features

Golgo 13 is as feature-packed as any game available for the NES. Play occurs in several different modes. In Horizontal Action scenes, the screen scrolls right and left only. It's used for walking through the city and some buildings, and in the dogfight and underwater sequences. Action is displayed from the viewpoint of someone watching Duke and the others interact. Pan & Zoom mode is used when Golgo 13 is surprised by a group of enemy agents. It shows the attackers from Duke's perspective. The Action Pass Maze mode happens in mazes that Duke must explore, and shows the walls surrounding him as well as the objects and enemies he encounters.

The sniper scenes (Pan & Zoom) are particularly exciting and well executed. While Duke is strolling around (Horizontal Action), however, you'll quickly discover that although he can kneel, he can't shoot from that position. This makes things unusually tough for him, since virtually all his assailants shoot from a kneeling position.

When play begins, Duke has full life force but no bullets. Both can be replenished if he finds special objects or defeats a powerful enemy.

Sound and Graphics

Excellent sound effects (explosion, kicks, and gunfire) and music. The "secret agent" theme song adds to the game's suspense. The graphics are impressive and show superb attention to detail. The animation is also very good.

Challenge

It's easy to make good progress through Golgo 13, particularly after you've practiced and made whatever maps and notes you can. Although 52 Continues sounds like a lot, it's still a rude surprise when you go beyond that number and suddenly find yourself back at the start of the game.

Play Value

Golgo 13 is a big game with loads of clues to find and areas to explore. It will take strategy, careful mapping, and many hours of practice to complete the game.

Tips, Tricks, and Strategies

- Use rapid fire selectively with Golgo 13. Your bullets aren't unlimited, so try not to waste them. In areas where there are big ammunition rewards for destroying enemies, you don't have to be as careful.
- Shoot everyone you see. Your bullets won't harm friends.

- In Pan & Zoom mode, aim a little high at snipers and shoot them first—not the helicopters. If you leave them alive, they'll defeat you quickly.
- If you hold still, the helicopters and frogmen in Pan & Zoom mode will usually come to you.
- Shoot incoming missiles before they explode to avoid damage to yourself.
- To defeat Rolling Thunder, just shoot it as many times and as quickly as you can.
- The closer you are to the jet fighters, the more damage your bullets seem to cause.
- Duke's rendezvous in the hotel restores his life points.
- To avoid losing life force unnecessarily, swim over or under the underwater mines.
- Avoid the octopuses unless your bullet supply is high.
- In the mazes, try to find the binoculars before wandering through the laser beams. Make sure all beams are off before going through. You can sometimes slip through a hole in the center of the beams, but it's much riskier.
- Maximum ammunition is 400 bullets. If you're fully stocked, don't pick up extra ammunition that you find. Wait until it's needed.

If you've given up on Golgo 13, see "Super Secrets" for more tips.

Gotcha!

Classification	Arcade
Players	1
Controller	Zapper and std. controller
Pause	Yes
Restart at Last Level	No
Manufacturer	LJN Toys, Inc.
Retail Price	$45.00

Ratings

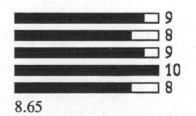

Instructions	9
Features	8
Graphics	9
Sound	10
Challenge	8
Play Value	8.65

☐ Gotcha!

Review

Gotcha! is a game of "Capture the Flag" played with guns that shoot paint pellets. Each side has a flag at its end of the playing area (the home base). The object is to be the first to steal the other side's flag and move it to your home base.

As you move about the playing area, opponents—controlled by the NES—will pop up and try to shoot you. If you shoot first and your aim is accurate, a blotch of paint will mark the enemy's chest. If you're too slow, he'll shoot you. If you're shot three times, run out of paint pellets, or the time clock runs out, the game ends. If you're running out of paint pellets, you can get more by shooting ammunition boxes that appear here and there, or by hitting an enemy who is carrying an ammunition box.

Gotcha! is played with the Zapper light gun in one hand and a standard controller in the other. Use the gun to shoot at the enemies, and the controller to scroll the screen right and left.

There are three difficulty levels (beginner, intermediate, and advanced), and three playing areas (forest, the Bronx, and winter). If you complete all areas, they repeat again.

Instructions

The instruction manual does a good job of describing the game and its rules. It won't make much sense, however, until you've played a few games.

Features

Since there are only three areas in the game, a Continue option would have been pointless. Having three difficulty levels helps keep the game interesting and challenging.

I'd have liked a few more features to spice things up, though. A paint grenade that, when hit, would take out all the enemies on screen would have been interesting. Also, a few more areas would have helped.

Sound and Graphics

I like the music for Gotcha! It makes me think of secret agents, and sets the proper mood. The only sound effect is the noise of gunshots. The scenery and characters are well designed and clearly drawn.

Challenge

It will take most players several rounds before they get the hang of Gotcha! Once you get used to the light gun and learn when its best to shoot and best to move on, play gets a lot more fun.

If it gets too easy at the beginner level (and it will if you practice), try the next level. You'll only have time for two shots at each enemy before you get blasted. The advanced level is for Wyatt Earp clones only. If you're extremely good, you may be able to get off one shot before the enemy opens fire. Make it count!

Of the three areas, winter is the toughest. Many of the enemies lie down in the snow to take a bead on you—offering a much smaller target.

Play Value

Success at Gotcha! requires the ability to manipulate two controllers at once, although only the control pad is used on the standard controller (for moving right and left). The hardest part of the game is being accurate while suffering the eye strain that comes from sighting down the Zapper's barrel with one eye squeezed shut. If you need a break, don't forget the Pause option.

It's nice to see new games that use the Zapper. It gets boring shooting ducks after awhile.

Tips, Tricks, and Strategies

- Don't hang around your own base. Unless you keep moving to the right, you'll never win.
- You don't have to shoot everyone. Any time things get too tough or you're running low on ammunition, try scrolling some of the enemies off the screen.
- If the blinking crosshairs appear, someone is about to shoot you. Shoot fast or prepare to move.

- If you're having trouble hitting things, try aiming a little high.
- Don't linger around the enemy's base camp. If you take too long, enemies will keep popping up to make you run out of ammo. Shoot them all quickly, shoot the flag, and then move away as fast as you can.
- Bonus points are given at the end of each round for the number of shots remaining and the unused time on the clock. Move quickly for bigger points.

Guerrilla War

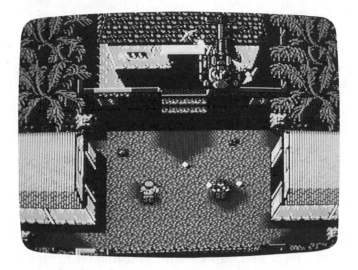

Classification	Arcade
Players	1 or 2 simultaneous
Controller	Standard
Pause	Yes
Restart at Last Level	Yes
Manufacturer	SNK Corp. of America
Retail Price	$44.95

Ratings

Instructions	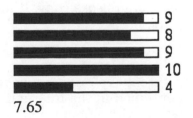	9
Features		8
Graphics		9
Sound		10
Challenge		4
Play Value	7.65	

Review

In Guerrilla War, it's you versus the enemy army in ten scenarios (jungle, farm village, coal mine, city, sewers, and so on). As the world's foremost guerrilla fighter, you are armed with a machine gun and an unlimited supply of hand grenades. Nine different power-up items can be found to improve your weaponry, clear the screen of enemies, increase your score, or add an extra life. Power-ups are obtained by destroying an enemy or an obstacle, or simply by finding them.

The enemy is well armed and has a host of ingenious weapons at its disposal. Tanks, trains, helicopters, and bulldozers will all try to crush the life from you. How fast can you move? Can you find the weapons you'll need to survive? Special tanks (marked with an IN sign) are available for your use. They offer more protection and fire-power, but—like you—are still subject to destruction.

Complicating things, the enemy holds many of your comrades captive. They've been tied up and placed in the field of battle to slow your progress. You can rescue them by touching them or running over them with the tank. Shoot them and you'll lose points. Don't be surprised when the enemy uses the hostages for cover.

Instructions

The instructions (like the game) are simple and straightforward. No discussion of plot is offered because there isn't one. As the manual states: *This is a shooting game. So go shoot something already. Note: The instruction manual reviewed was a pre-release copy. It may change somewhat in the final version.*

Features

There are three levels of play: easy, normal, and hard. Although mentioned in the instructions, it will take some experimentation with the buttons to set the level. They should have been made more accessible, perhaps included in a main menu, or at least explained better.

The weaponry is varied and interesting, and includes three-way/split bullets, high-power grenades, and several bombs and explosives. The high-powered weapons like the flamethrower are the most fun.

Sound and Graphics

Super sound effects (explosions and gunfire). The music is also very good, and changes depending on the area you're in.

The scenery and backgrounds are exceptionally sharp. The characters—perhaps because of their petite size—are indistinct and fuzzy. Another war in the land of the Lilliputians . . .

Challenge

In addition to unlimited Continues, Guerrilla War makes things even easier. Instead of starting over at the beginning of the last level, you start at the exact spot where you last died! Not only that, but whoever you were last fighting— including the super enemies—retains the number of hits it has taken so far. All you need is persistence to defeat even the toughest foes.

Once you've made it through the entire game, try a more difficult level. If you want to add some challenge, play only until you die or until you die a set number of times. See how far you can get with this self-imposed limit.

Play Value

What's special about Guerrilla War is that it can be finished by almost anyone within a few hours. If you have kids and don't mind their playing war games, let them try this one. Theme aside, the ear-to-ear grin that accompanies completing an NES game is worth seeing. (Just don't tell them that you beat it, too!)

Note: Check out the opening screens. I never thought I'd see Che Guevera's face in a game.

Tips, Tricks, and Strategies

- Go for the yellow and red soldiers. They hide power-up items. Barricades occasionally do, too.
- Don't use your tank to shoot the bridge in the first area. If you do, you'll have to get out and walk. (You'll find another tank waiting for you at the other end, though.)
- Try to save a tank for the helicopter attack at the end of the first scenario. It makes things a lot easier. [ES]
- On the ship, the huge gunners that pop up out of the hold are best attacked from the side, not the front.
- Right after picking up a C (clearing bomb), toss a hand grenade to destroy all the enemies on screen. K symbols have a similar effect.

Hoops

Classification	Sports
Players	1 or 2 simultaneous
Controller	Standard
Pause	Yes
Restart at Last Level	Two-on-two mode only
Manufacturer	Jaleco USA, Inc.
Retail Price	$42.95

Ratings

Instructions	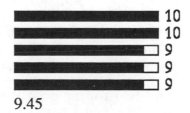	10
Features		10
Graphics		9
Sound		9
Challenge		9
Play Value	9.45	

Review

Hoops is schoolyard basketball, played on a half court. It's you against the toughest players in the neighborhood. To win, you have to be able to shoot accurately, block, rebound, and steal the ball whenever the opportunity arises. Every player, no matter how short, can do a slam dunk if close enough to the basket. Score is kept on the back wall of the court using chalk marks.

Instructions

Although the manual I had for Hoops was a typewritten draft rather than a final production copy, it was well written and complete. Once graphics are added, there should be little question about game options or how to play.

Features

Hoops has an outstanding number of play options. In one-player games, you can play one-on-one Shoot for Possession or Around the World, or two-on-two Tournament Play or Shoot for Possession. In two-player games, both players can team together and play against the computer, or play against each other (one-on-one or two-on-two). Tournament Play, either with the players teaming up or against each other, is also available. In all games there are four rules that, when broken, cause a change in possession of the ball: traveling, charging, pushing, and throwing or shooting the ball out of bounds.

For each game, players select the score to be played to (10, 15, 20, or 25), a "losers out" or "winners out" game (who gets possession of the ball after a basket is scored), and whether it will be played in a court on the east or west side of the city. Teams are chosen from a roster of eight players (men and women), each with different playing styles and strengths.

In two-on-two Tournament Play, each time your team wins you will be given a password to continue the tournament at a later time without losing your spot in the standings. If you win 15 games, there is a special ending sequence.

Hoops also has a Watch mode where you can check out the players and the game as the NES plays against itself.

Sound and Graphics

I was impressed with the graphics in Hoops. Although there are only two different play areas (east- and west-side courts), I like the detail in the court and background—right down to the graffiti on the walls.

The music is fun-time sports stuff, and fits well with the game. Like most NES songs, however, it can become tedious. Sound effects are accurately done, and include the sounds made by the ball as it's dribbled and as it bounces off the backboard.

Challenge

Around the World—where it's just you against the computer—is extremely tough. The computer player rarely misses, so you'll have to be very accurate to just remain even. Being good at Around the World won't help much in Shoot for Possession games, however, so practice accordingly.

From my experience, the toughest part of the game is getting close enough to try a slam dunk without losing the ball. In two-on-two play, pick your teammates wisely so you'll balance each other's strengths and weaknesses.

Two-on-two games, especially those where you're the only player, add the challenge of simultaneously trying to control both members of a team. It's easier—and frequently more fun—to play two-on-two if a friend controls the second member of the team.

Play Value

Hoops, particularly in two-player mode, is challenging and a lot of fun. Once you've gained sufficient skill to totally embarrass your friends, it's time to move on to the one-player games.

Tips, Tricks, and Strategies

■ You can also steal the ball while pressing B, not just A. If you aren't careful, however, your player will shoot from wherever he's currently standing as soon as he gains possession of the ball.

■ Try shooting from different parts of the court. Many players have their own preferred "hit zones."

■ Like many sports games where there's 360-degree play control and frequent movements, the standard NES controller may give you more thumb action than you'll find comfortable. Try a joystick if you get sore.

■ To avoid disappointment and discouragement, it's easiest to learn Hoops by playing with a friend. Until you really know what you're doing, the computer players will stomp you into the dust.

Karnov

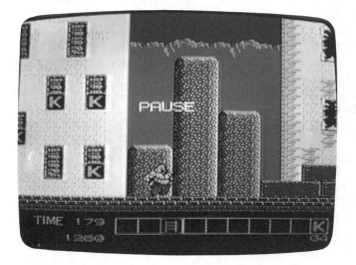

Classification	Arcade
Players	1
Controller	Standard
Pause	Yes
Restart at Last Level	Yes
Manufacturer	Data East USA, Inc.
Retail Price	$44.95

Ratings

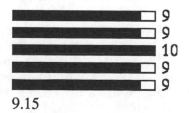

Instructions	9
Features	9
Graphics	10
Sound	9
Challenge	9
Play Value	9.15

Review

Jinborov Karnovski ("Karnov" for short) is a former circus strongman with an unusual talent. He can shoot fireballs from his mouth.

An evil dragon has ransacked Karnov's village and stolen the wondrous Treasure of Babylon. As game-type dragon's are known to do, it has left behind a bevy of monsters to make things tough for Karnov and the people of the village. As Karnov, your mission (Can you guess?) is to make your way through nine stages of play, defeat the monsters, and reclaim the treasure.

Instructions

The instructions are clearly written. Everything needed to play the game is here, as well as a few moderately helpful tips. There are a lot of monsters in Karnov, yet the manual only gives you a peek at five of them.

Features

Although many of the monsters can easily be knocked off with fireballs, Karnov has ten special powers that can make his quest simpler. A ladder, wings, and magic jumping boots help him reach greater heights. A shield can protect him from the most viscious attacks. Bombs, boomerangs, and a thunder clapper can be used to handle the really tough monsters.

The trick, though, is that to use the powers, you have to find them. Most wear off after a short time, some are available only in certain areas, and many disappear after they've been used. To make things a little easier, however, several of the powers can be stockpiled. They remain with you as long as you use the Continue option.

The only feature I'd like to see changed is the way you select a special power when you want to use one. The available powers are shown on screen at all times. Whenever you use the control pad to move Karnov left or right, the special power selector also moves left or right. To choose one, you must highlight it and press the Select button. Unfortunately, getting to the right one before Karnov gets wiped out is frequently a matter of life and death. It's much harder than it might be if the control pad wasn't being used for double duty.

Sound and Graphics

Great music and sound effects—with the exception of Karnov's fire balls. They sound like radio static.

Karnov has some of the best graphics around. It has imaginative scenery and bizarre monsters . . . all drawn with exceptional detail (right down to the Lizard Man's tiny scales).

Challenge

With unlimited Continues, progress is possible in Karnov, but it usually comes only after playing each Stage many times. It will often take that many tries to find the best route and determine how each monster should be handled. Once you've advanced about halfway through a Stage, however, you can continue from that point rather than having to start at its beginning whenever Karnov dies.

Play Value

Karnov is a great arcade game. Although the plot is no more imaginative than any of the other NES arcade games, the design of the characters and landscape *definitely* is. No matter how many times I've played it, it's always fun to come back to.

Tips, Tricks, and Strategies

- Some special powers only appear after defeating certain monsters. Keep your eyes open.
- Don't forget to take your ladder with you. It comes along automatically if you climb down to the ground, but not if you jump off. If you do jump, climb back up it a little ways and back down again to retrieve it.
- Karnov can shoot while on the ladder. If you take advantage of this ability, you can avoid some of the game's toughest confrontations.

■ Karnov doesn't need the swimming mask to go under-
water, but it does speed him up.
■ Don't pass up an opportunity to pick up easy K's. Al-
though they obviously aren't as critical as weapons, if
you collect 50, Karnov gets an extra life.
■ To defeat the flying dragon, you have to shoot it in the
head.
■ There are trees that you can climb in Stage 3.
■ Jumping into a hole doesn't always mean death for
Karnov. For example, there's a K bonanza in Stage 3 if
you go underground in the right spot.
■ You can use the boomerang to soften up any dinosaurs
you meet.
■ There are a dozen or so bombs hidden at the start of
Stage 4. See if you can make them appear.
■ Duck down and shoot to dispatch the knights at the start
of Stage 6.

If you've given up on Karnov, see "Super Secrets" for
more tips.

Lee Trevino's Fighting Golf

Classification	Sports
Players	1 to 4
Controller	Standard
Pause	Not applicable
Restart at Last Level	Not applicable
Manufacturer	SNK Corp. of America
Retail Price	$42.95

Ratings

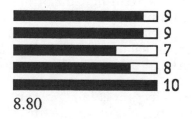

Instructions	9
Features	9
Graphics	7
Sound	8
Challenge	10
Play Value	8.80

Review

If you're ready to play with the big boys (or be one of the big boys), limber up your swinging finger for Lee Trevino's Fighting Golf! The game allows up to four players to be Lee Trevino ("Super Mex"), Pretty Amy, Big Jumbo (the long ball hitter), or Miracle Chosuke (perfecter of the "reverse miracle putt"). Play is on a tough U.S. course or a water, hazard-filled Japanese course.

Other than putting, it takes three presses of the A button to complete a stroke: one to start it, one to finish the backswing, and one to complete the follow-through. If you time the follow-through correctly, you can also draw or fade the ball. By pressing up or down on the control pad while swinging, you can hit the ball high or keep it low to the ground.

What I find amazing about this game is that, just like in real life, I shoot triple bogeys and three-putt half the greens. My unusual swing and lack of direction seem to curse me here, too.

Instructions

The instructions are thorough and explain everything that's needed to play the game. A few details—like which clubs can successfully be used under what circumstances, however—are left for you to discover. A basic understanding of golf helps.

Features

Lee Trevino's Fighting Golf offers an impressive feature list. Up to four players can play a U.S. or Japanese course, standard or Nassau game. There are four playing styles to choose from, each represented by a different golfer. If you care to take a few swings before going out, there's even a practice tee.

Club selection is fairly complete. Notably, only the 2-wood and iron are omitted—in favor of the 1-iron. Frankly, I'm a bit surprised at this. After being struck by lightning on two separate occasions, Lee Trevino, stuck in the middle of a fairway during a thunderstorm, reportedly was seen waving a 1-iron over his head. When asked why, he said, "Even God can't hit a 1-iron!"

In addition to choosing clubs and direction, players can play draw and fade shots, hit high or low, and apply backspin. While choosing a direction, players can view the immediate area, the entire hole, or take a peek at the green. The NES automatically recommends a club and direction for each shot.

On the down side, proper club choice seems to be based on distance, rather than on the ball's lie. For example, the computer-generated player is somehow able to play a driver from the rough. (You think maybe he has a tee in his pocket? I haven't caught anyone improving a lie with his foot yet, but I'm keeping my eyes open.)

Sound and Graphics

The graphics are okay for a game of this sort, but lack the detail found in most current games. One nice touch is that the players sometimes express joy, disappointment, and anger, depending on what happened to the current shot.

The sound effects are largely limited to the splash of the ball landing in one of the many water obstacles and the rustling of leaves or a ricochet as the ball fails to clear a tree. The theme music is relaxing—kind of pastoral—and is appropriate for a golf game.

Challenge

If you're a golfer, think back to your worst round (if you haven't already blotted it from your memory). Now add 50 strokes. If real golf had proven as tough as Lee Trevino's Fighting Golf, I would have given up years ago.

Coordination and timing, as in the real game, are key. Hitting a good shot requires three separate, accurately timed presses of the A button. Doing it consistently is what separates the great golfers from the also-rans (myself included). If you have the time, however, birdies, pars, and bogeys will come more often. Personally, I think my short game needs work.

If humiliation is your thing, try playing Nassau with a randomly selected opponent. You'll find more often than not that any opponent, hits perfect 260-yard tee shots, frequently chips in from 75 yards out, and one-putts almost every green. To be fair, each usually has at least one bad hole out of nine.

Unless your reflexes are really sharp, play by yourself or against a friend. It's not nearly so embarrassing when you're both hitting into the water, trees, or bunkers at least twice each hole.

Play Value

The basic rules of golf, as well as physical laws (gravity, the effect of wind, what happens when you hit a tree), all appear to apply. Good shots feel almost as good as ones made on a real course. Although it doesn't beat the real thing, the game gives you an opportunity to try out two really tough courses for about the price of two rounds on a public course (one round with cart rental and lunch). Bottom line: Lee Trevino's Fighting Golf is frustrating, but fun.

Tips, Tricks, and Strategies

■ Try out the different players. Each has his or her own strengths and weaknesses.
■ The direction automatically selected for each shot seems to be based on the shortest path to the green. As in golf, this isn't always the best approach. Adjust direction as necessary.
■ The clubs that the NES selects for you, particularly the irons, are often correct only if you hit a perfect all-out shot. If you find that you're frequently short, try a longer iron or a wood.
■ Learn to master the fade and draw shots. They're very helpful for playing around trees.
■ If only a perfect shot will take you over a water hazard or bunker, try playing short or going around.
■ Take advantage of the wind when you can. Play the shot high, for example, if there's a strong following wind.
■ It's hard to press A fast enough on a short approach shot to keep from over-shooting the green. If you're just off the edge of the green, try a putter.
■ For really short putts, set A to rapid fire. It's the only way I know of to hit the button fast enough. (Be sure to set it back after the shot or you'll blow your next drive!)

The Legend of Zelda

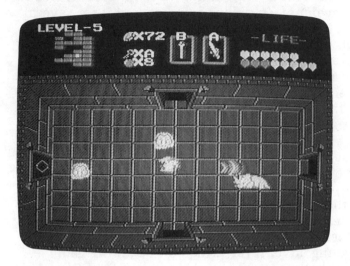

Classification	Adventure
Players	1
Controller	Standard
Pause	Yes
Restart at Last Level	Yes, via battery backup
Manufacturer	Nintendo of America, Inc.
Retail Price	$34.95

Ratings

Instructions	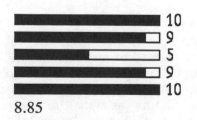	10
Features		9
Graphics		5
Sound		9
Challenge		10
Play Value	8.85	

Review

The Legend of Zelda has maintained its high ranking among NES games for a long time now. Although it's weak graphically, Legend of Zelda has remained a hit for several reasons. First, it's an adventure in every sense of the word. Being a tough player with good reflexes helps, but it isn't enough. There are scores of clues to be unraveled, and secret passages and special objects that must be found.

Second, the game is extremely challenging. Even with all the hints that the manual provides, the game offers days (or weeks) of exciting play. And after finishing the adventure, there's a second one that's built in!

Finally, it's one of the few cartridges that includes a built-in "Save Game" option. Although serving the same purpose as a password, you can continue the game after shutting off the NES with considerably less bother than having to enter the typical 10- to 25-character password required by other games.

As the young adventurer Link, you begin the game with a simple shield, a sword, and three hearts of life. (As you build experience, Link's heart potential increases accordingly.) The object of the game is to recover the eight missing pieces of the mystical Triforce of wisdom and defeat Ganon, the evil prince that has captured Princess Zelda. The Triforce pieces have been hidden in the underground caverns of Hyrule and are guarded by an assortment of evil creatures. So find the pieces quickly and make your way to Death Mountain—where Ganon awaits your arrival.

Instructions

The instructions for Legend of Zelda are the most complete and hint-packed of any NES game. Actually, it goes overboard in this respect. There are so many hints that you may find, at some point, you're spending as much time with the manual as with the game. Also included is a fold-out map that shows the layout of the land of Hyrule (where the adventure takes place), describes some of the creatures you'll meet and the weapons you can obtain, and offers still more playing tips.

Features

There are many special items in the land of Hyrule. Finding, or, in some cases, buying them and learning their secrets contribute in large part to the game's continued play value. Some of the more useful items include boomerangs, bombs, bait (for luring the enemy creatures), a ladder, and the raft. Of course, many items are magical and convey considerably more power to their owner than the garden variety weapons.

The ability to throw his sword is key to keeping Link alive. Throwing the sword allows him to attack most monsters from a safe distance. Unfortunately, the first time Link is even scratched by an adversary (reducing his heart strength), he must resort to face-to-face combat. This leads you on an almost constant search for hearts and fairies (to restore his hearts). It might have been better if he at least retained throwing power until the first complete heart had been lost.

There's no need to mess with passwords in the Legend of Zelda. There's a battery inside the cartridge that remembers where you left off in the adventure and the weapons that have been accumulated. Up to three separate game records can be stored. There are also unlimited Continues during normal play.

Sound and Graphics

The graphics are the Legend of Zelda's greatest weakness. Particularly in the outerworld, Link and the creatures he meets are a bit too much like Munchkins and Muppets to evoke any real feelings of fear. Everything—including Link—seems a few sizes too small. The underworld, although suffering from the same character design weakness, has much more detail in the backgrounds and stronger graphics in general.

The music is good, especially the haunting tune played in the dungeon and the one used for the opening screens. The outerworld music is more cartoonish and wears thin quickly. The sound effects are handled well.

Challenge

Legend of Zelda is extremely challenging. To win the pieces of the Triforce, you have to conquer each of the underworld labyrinths of Hyrule. But you have to find them first! Each time Link dies during an attempt, he is returned to the game's starting point. To continue in the same labyrinth, he must first make his way there again.

Beating the ruling monsters of each labyrinth requires excellent timing, coordination, and a willingness to explore different strategies using a number of weapons and special objects. There's no telling what will work best—or at all—until you try it.

Play Value

Newer games have more impressive graphics and monsters than the Legend of Zelda, but it continues to be a favorite of many players.

Tips, Tricks, and Strategies

- Try to fight long-distance whenever possible. If the enemy can't touch you, you can't lose life points as easily. If you can't fight from a distance, try sneaking up from behind.
- Be careful when you play with fire. You, too, can get burned. By the way, the candle can also be used to burn bushes, as well as light up dark rooms.
- Depending on where an enemy dies, some bonus objects left behind may be out of reach. Try retrieving them with a special object.
- Docks and rafts aren't the same thing. You can't do anything on a dock unless you also have a raft.
- Not everything can be purchased. Don't leave the labyrinths without searching them thoroughly. Weapons and special objects are hidden there.
- Try pushing things in the labyrinths. That and blowing holes in the walls will lead you to some interesting spots. For this reason, it's a good idea to stock up on bombs before going into the labyrinths.

- The blue ring must be purchased in a secret room hidden beneath an Armos. *[GJ]*
- Enter the waterfall for directions to the white sword. *[GJ]*
- Bombs can be used to stun the Dodongos, softening them up for Link's sword. If you drop the bombs close enough, the Dodongos will eat them and explode on their own. *[GJ]*
- Use bombs on Manhandia. Be sure to hit its center. *[GJ]*
- Aquamentus is best attacked from afar by repeatedly shooting Link's sword, or by attacking and retreating, attacking and retreating. *[GJ]*
- You can destroy the floating Patra by going for the encircling ones first, followed by the larger one in the center. *[GJ]*
- Gleeok is only affected by attacks to its necks or heads. *[GJ]*

If you've given up on the Legend of Zelda, see "Super Secrets" for more tips.

Legendary Wings

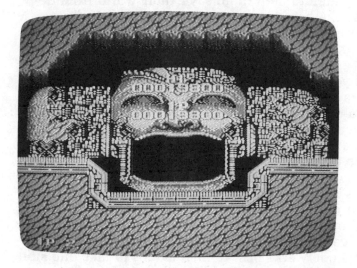

Classification	Arcade
Players	1 or 2 simultaneous
Controller	Standard
Pause	Yes
Restart at Last Level	Yes, if earned
Manufacturer	Capcom USA, Inc.
Retail Price	$34.95

Ratings

Instructions		5
Features		9
Graphics		10
Sound		9
Challenge		10
Play Value	8.60	

91

Review

In Legendary Wings, Ares (the God of War) has given wings to two young men to help them save their world from destruction. As the hero (or heroes), it's your task to fly about, building up power and destroying anything that stands in your way. Not much of a plot, but it is just an arcade game.

At first your power is limited to a single-shot gun and a cannon. As you find power-up items (up to a maximum of four), you obtain progressively more destructive weapons and defensive powers. Each time you're hit, weapons and powers are reduced. Game controls are simple: Button A shoots the cannon and B fires the gun.

Two-player simultaneous play is supported, but you may find it's more trouble than it's worth. When the action gets fast and furious, it's hard to tell one player's character from the other—even though each is a different color. Also, if one gets swallowed by the giant head, you both do. Two-player mode works best if each agrees to take one side of the screen, and allows as little overlap as possible.

Instructions

The manual is weak. Beyond describing how the controls operate and the bonuses and powers that are available, you're on your own. The enemy characters are displayed and named, but no additional details are supplied—such as where you'll meet them, their individual attacking style and powers, or how you might defeat them.

Features

There are both horizontal and vertically scrolling play areas. The main game area moves vertically. In those areas both the cannon and gun are available to you. In the horizontal stages (bonus areas and danger zones), only the gun may be used.

Legendary Wings has many powers that can be obtained. Unfortunately, the lower-level ones are lost the second your character gets hit. Too fleeting for my taste . . . Another feature I don't care for is the way scores are displayed. They are only visible when you pause the game or lose. On the other hand, it certainly doesn't distract you or clutter up the screen.

Continues are not automatic; they must be earned in the Bonus zones. Of course, they're only useful if you've advanced beyond the first stage.

Sound and Graphics

Nice theme music and sound effects (explosions and gunfire). I'm not sure who dreamed up the "Love Boat" music that plays at the end of each game, though. It's not really appropriate and seems to trivialize your play.

The graphics are clear and colorful, and the monsters are imaginative. The Danger Zone inside the giant head is a little too realistic and a bit disgusting. Don't step on his intestines . . .

Challenge

I played Legendary Wings a long time before I made it beyond the first half of stage 1. It took one of the tips below before I discovered why my character was constantly dying at the last moment. Not much strategy is required. If you have sharp reflexes and a good aim, you have a chance of doing all right in Legendary Wings.

Play Value

If you don't give up after repeatedly being killed off in stage 1, you'll probably enjoy Legendary Wings. No plot, but lots of arcade action.

Tips, Tricks, and Strategies

- In the first scenario, you can shoot the heads on the statues if you pick them off before they begin to fly. In general, though, it's a sucker move. You'll usually lose a life or two this way. It's easier just to dodge them.
- Not all whirlwinds are evil. If you let the small ones carry you inside, you'll be rewarded with enormous bonus points and powers. There's one in each stage.
- Continues can be found in the bonus stages. They're useless, of course, unless you've completed Stage 1.

☐ Legendary Wings

- Don't drag your feet in the bonus stages. It's easy to get trapped behind walls and lose a life.
- Anything in the first three stages that tries to shoot you or run into you (except the giant head) can be destroyed. Certain monsters must be destroyed to complete a stage. [GJ]
- Once you become a firebird, you can usually go an area or two before losing any power. [GJ]
- A controller with rapid-fire is almost a necessity if you want to get anywhere in Legendary Wings.

If you've given up on Legendary Wings, see "Super Secrets" for more tips.

Mappy-Land

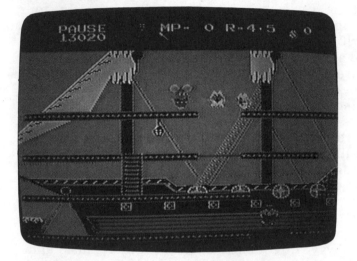

Classification	Kids' Game
Players	1
Controller	Standard
Pause	Yes
Restart at Last Level	Yes
Manufacturer	Taxan USA Corporation
Retail Price	$42.95

Ratings

Instructions	8
Features	9
Graphics	6
Sound	10
Challenge	6
Play Value	7.75

Review

Mappy-Land is one of a handful of games created for young children. The theme is a pleasant one: Help Mappy the mouse find the hidden presents. Mappy-Land contains four stories or stages. In story 1, you'll have to find some cheese for your girlfriend Mapico's birthday party. In story 2, you must locate a ring for your wedding. You'll have to find a Christmas tree in story 3. In the last story, your search is for a ball for your son Mappy Jr.'s birthday party.

Each stage has eight areas to be explored. They include scenes from a pirate ship, a jungle, an old western town, a railroad, and more. To complete each area, Mappy must find all of the presents that have been hidden there and then make his way through the doorway at the far right. In some areas, an additional object is needed to pass through the door. If Mappy finds the exit blocked, he must look for the secret entrance to a special sub-area. It's there that the extra object can be found.

Mappy's way is frequently obstructed by Nyamco and the Mukies (kittens), members of the Guchi Gang. If they touch him, he spins dizzily across the screen and loses a life. Mappy can drop toys and other objects to distract the gang. There are also weapons in each area—like punching bags, pulleys, bowling balls, and horizontal bars—that Mappy can use to knock the gang members down.

Each area is divided into several levels. Mappy can move from level to level by climbing ladders and bouncing on strategically placed trampolines. However, his trampoline jumps are limited. If he bounces too many times, the trampoline will give way and Mappy will lose another life.

Instructions

The instruction manual does a reasonable job of describing the game without going into a lot of detail. It talks about the different characters, for example, but never shows them. Luckily, they're all illustrated at the end of the game demo.

Features

One option that children should welcome is the game's provision for starting at any odd-numbered area within stages 1 through 4. This means if they get stuck on an earlier stage or area, they can still jump ahead and see what the higher-numbered areas look like. There are also unlimited Continues in Mappy-Land. Once you've devised a strategy to clear an area, you can continue until you finally get it right.

Sound and Graphics

The music and sound effects in Mappy-Land are excellent. The graphics, unfortunately, aren't as good. Most drawings show little detail and the choice of colors at times interferes with the game. While they are bright and beautiful, the colors and designs occasionally make it hard to see all the objects hidden in the background.

Challenge

The areas in stage 1 are all fairly easy. When your kids (or you) have mastered this stage, there are three more levels of difficulty to keep them entertained. The toughest areas are the jungles, particularly the ones in stages 3 and 4. The trampolines float free and Mappy must bounce from one to another to get anywhere. The secret sub-area within the jungle is a dark cave. It's so dark, in fact, that you can't see where the ladders or trampolines are!

Play Value

Mappy-Land is a great game for kids. Although teenagers will probably find it too tame, adults may appreciate it. It's a nonviolent game that takes planning and practice to master.

Tips, Tricks, and Strategies

■ Weapons for Protection are used in reverse of the order in which they were found. The next one to be used will be the one farthest to the right. Make sure the one you're about to use is correct for the enemy that is approaching.

■ Watch the color of the trampoline change as Mappy bounces. If it becomes red, he'll fall through and lose a life. If there's another trampoline below that one, however, he'll keep bouncing.
■ The bowling ball always rolls to the right. The pulleys always slide to the left.
■ If you swing on the horizontal bars, you can catch enemies on your level and the one above.
■ Watch for Weapons of Protection to appear where Mappy just lost a life. Sometimes picking up an item will also make them appear nearby.
■ If you want to load up on fish in the Jungle World in stage 1–4, hang out at the bottom of the first or second set of vines.
■ If Mappy takes too long finding the presents in an area, a nasty creature will come for him. When the music speeds up, it's time to go.
■ It takes two special items to get across the bridge in stage 4-3. Make sure you find them both.
■ Try climbing the vines in the jungle all the way to the top. Some will give you a surprise.

If you've given up on Mappy-Land, see "Super Secrets" for more tips.

Marble Madness

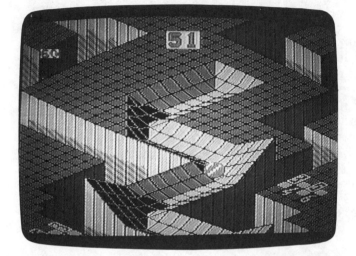

Classification	Arcade
Players	1 or 2 simultaneous
Controller	Standard
Pause	Yes
Restart at Last Level	No
Manufacturer	Milton Bradley Company
Retail Price	$40 approx.

Ratings

Instructions	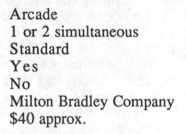	10
Features		8
Graphics		10
Sound		9
Challenge		8
Play Value	8.85	

Review

In Marble Madness, you must guide a marble through six increasingly complex 3-D mazes. In each maze you'll find narrow ramps, 90-degree angles, and a variety of tiny creatures that attempt to stop your forward progress.

Each maze must be completed in a specific amount of time. If you lose a marble (by falling off the maze, jumping too far and breaking it, or getting thumped by an enemy), a new one is constructed for you, but the clock ticks on. Point and time bonuses are scattered liberally throughout Marble Madness, but it's up to you to find them.

Instructions

No problems here. The instructions, like the game, are simple and clearly explained. Some additional hints on bonuses would have been helpful, though.

Features

In addition to running the mazes while trying not to fall off, there's the added wrinkle of having to avoid or battle the enemies that inhabit marble land. Two-player games add competition to the play. When one player gets ahead of the other, the lagging marble is moved forward far enough to catch up and is assessed a time penalty.

There are three feature-related problems: two of implementation and one of omission. The first is that at the start of each new game you must reenter your name or initials. Doing this once is necessary to register high scores, but why force the player to do it over and over? Having the main menu offer Start and Continue options would have handled this nicely.

Second, if one player runs out of time in a two-player game, the screen is temporarily frozen. When it unfreezes, there's a good chance that the remaining player's marble will move in some direction other than the one he or she wanted to go.

The problem of omission is that there is no way to continue from the last level. Marble Madness is so difficult that many may never see the higher levels without being able to Continue.

Sound and Graphics

The 3-D graphics, done in "computer grid style," are impressive. The sound effects and music are also effective.

Challenge

Marble Madness is primarily a test of eye/hand coordination. Teens tend to do well at it. Adults, on the other hand, with their slower reaction times and—from my own experience—difficulty making subtle movements, don't fare as well.

Play Value

Marble Madness is fun, if occasionally maddening, to play. Once all six levels have been beaten, teens can keep playing for higher scores. Without more levels, however, it's not clear that they'll continue to be interested in the game.

Tips, Tricks, and Strategies

■ At the beginning of each game, you can choose to hold the controller horizontally (90 degrees)—the normal way—or diagonally (45 degrees). The diagonal hold lets the control pad arrows make diagonal movements, instead of straight north, east, south, and west. Since many of the ramp angles are northeast, southwest, and so on, you may find the diagonal hold more productive.
■ Make heavy use of the A button for straightaways and any other areas that can be handled with gross movements. *[GJ]*
■ Near the end of the first race are two checkerboard patterns with numbers. If you can muster the speed, you can jump into either area for bonus points. You'll receive 1,000 points times the number you land on. If you land on an unnumbered area of the grid, you'll only get 1,000 points. *[RA], [GJ]*
■ You can complete the intermediate level by riding the wave or by taking the ramps (the long way). If you find the wave difficult to master, try going the long way. It's much easier.
■ Watch for the magic wand. If it's waved over your marble, you'll be granted extra time to complete the level.

- In the Silly Race, you receive three seconds of bonus time for squishing each little enemy (except the planes). *[GJ]*
- Most things are backwards in the Silly Race. Uphill is downhill and vice versa.
- In addition to playing for points, you're also playing for time. One way to get extra time is to play with a friend. His loss is your gain (and vice versa). *[GJ]*

Mega Man II

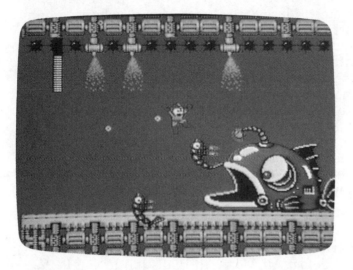

Classification	Arcade
Players	1
Controller	Standard
Pause	Yes
Restart at Last Level	Yes
Manufacturer	Capcom USA, Inc.
Retail Price	$49.95

Ratings

Instructions	████████████████████░	9
Features	██████████████████████	10
Graphics	██████████████████████	10
Sound	██████████████████████	10
Challenge	██████████████████████	10
Play Value	9.80	

Review

In the year 200X (that's one year after Clash at Demonhead, for those of you who are keeping track), Dr. Light created a super robot named Mega Man. Mega Man was built to help defend against the evil scientist Dr. Wiley. Well, Dr. Wiley is back. He has eight super robots of his own and he's itching for a fight.

Each super robot has its own area of the game. You can start in any of the eight areas, and select the order in which they're completed. Each time you destroy one of the super robots, Mega Man gains a new power that he can use for the rest of the game. As each super robot is beaten, its square is removed from the game's "area select" menu. One square, however, is always saved for last—the fight with Dr. Wiley.

Instructions

To get you started, the instructions provide step-by-step information to defeat Air Man. All that's left to you is the mechanics of moving through the area and shooting when you have to. The manual identifies many of the monsters you'll meet in Dr. Wiley's world, but tells nothing about them other than their names.

Features

Most games dictate the sequence of play to you. Not Mega Man II. In it, you determine the enemies to combat, in the order you prefer. If the game gets too easy (don't hold your breath waiting for this to happen), you can play at the higher difficulty level.

Although Mega Man's standard weapon works well for most monsters and even on some of the super robots, the special weapons he earns will prove invaluable. Some are more effective than others, depending on the monster he's attacking. Learning which weapon works best for each monster—big and small—is a major part of the game.

You can earn eight different powers, one for each super robot you conquer. There are also three vehicles that can be earned. They're critical in some areas. Even though the manual tells you what each power and vehicle is, you'll find it helpful to memorize the code letter or number for each one so you don't waste them by mistake. (The Select screen only identifies them by letter or number.)

There are unlimited Continues within Mega Man II, and a password option lets you continue after turning off the NES. Password restarts let Mega Man retain all super powers that have been earned, and keep track of the enemies that have been defeated.

Sound and Graphics

Sound and graphics don't get much better than this. Each area has a different musical theme. Some are so good that I actually found myself tapping my foot! The graphics are equally stunning, particularly the scenes with the sky and clouds in the background. Great stuff! Give those guys a raise.

Challenge

Although several of the levels are fairly easy (once you learn the tricks), levels become incredibly difficult as you progress. The final confrontation with Dr. Wiley is actually a series of confrontations. And they're mean and nasty— the scenarios and the creatures that live in them. Are you sure you're up for this? Just wait until you meet the Dragon and Guts-Dozer! The password for this level, by the way, will only start you at the first confrontation. I'd think twice about starting this phase unless you have at least half a day to spare.

Play Value

I predict that Mega Man II will be one of the hottest games of the year. The challenge level ranges from easy to super hard depending on the area you're in. The game can be beaten, but you'll have to invest a lot of time and energy first. Because the graphics, sound, and play are so exciting, you'll want to play Mega Man II again even after you've finally won. It's a great game!

Tips, Tricks, and Strategies

- Some enemies, particularly the small pesky ones, may best be left alone. If you and your weapons are already fully powered, don't waste your time with them. There's nothing to be gained.
- Special weapons can be used against almost any monster, not just the area bosses.
- To finish off the Hot Dogs before Mega Man gets toasted, it's merely a matter of timing your jumps correctly. Try to get off several shots with each jump to destroy them quicker.
- You can get past the first few Atomic Chickens in the Wood Man stage by hiding next to the ledges. They'll just leap over your head.
- Don't jump over Lantern Fish. Walk through them.
- Save up your energy crystals for your meeting with Metal Man.
- The Quick Man area is aptly named. There's no way through the laser beams other than being faster than they are. Plan your route carefully. An extra second here or there, and you're dead. (You might consider saving this area for last.)
- It's best to shoot the Hotheads from a distance.
- If you don't feel like wasting special weapons, you can hop over the jack-in-the-box.
- Energy crystals are extremely rare. (They're shaped like a box and have an E on them.) If you find one, save it until it's really needed. Be sure to use it before you lose your last life, though.
- The level of difficulty of the various areas is far from equal. If you're stuck in one, move on to another. (No sense wearing your button-pushing finger to a nub when there's an easier way.)
- Learn the difference between the elevator and levitation powers. To use the elevator, you must stand directly against a wall and point at it. Then just hop up onto the elevator platform. Levitation, however, must be done away from a wall. If you're too close to a wall, you'll just waste your power. (**Very Important Note:** *You can create three levitation platforms at one time.*)

◼ Learning to make effective use of the energy and weapons power capsules is very important. See "Super Secrets" if you haven't figured it out.
◼ Since you can't use a weapon while Mega Man's freeze power is being used, it's best for those times when you want to change position on screen in relative safety. If you touch a frozen monster, however, you can still be damaged.
◼ Rapid fire can be a big help with Mega Man II. If your controller has a turbo mode, set button B for it.

If you've given up on Mega Man II, see "Super Secrets" for more tips.

Metal Gear

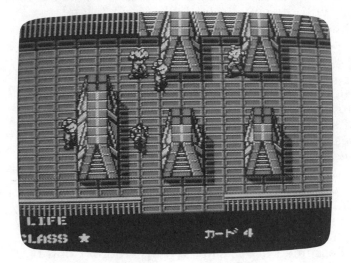

Classification	Arcade
Players	1
Controller	Standard
Pause	Yes
Restart at Last Level	Yes
Manufacturer	Ultra Software Corp.
Retail Price	$39.95

Ratings

Instructions	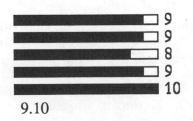	9
Features		9
Graphics		8
Sound		9
Challenge		10
Play Value	9.10	

Review

In this game, you play the role of Solid Snake (Who names these guys?), an ex-Marine whose mission is to destroy a super weapon with the equally unlikely name "Metal Gear." Metal Gear is hidden in a multileveled fortress within a city called Outer Heaven. To destroy it, you must make your way past guard dogs, security alarms, lasers, and a variety of heavily armed military personnel. Although you start with nothing more than a pack of cigarettes, a radio transceiver, and your bare hands, you'll find weapons and supplies along the way.

Metal Gear's onscreen captions are occasionally bizarre, filled with typos, and reminiscent of the type of Japanese-to-English translations you find in old Godzilla movies. "Oh, oh . . . the truck have started to move" was one of the better ones. One that initially tripped me up was that several guards say "I feel asleep" instead of "fell asleep." The former implies that he's groggy or just talking in his sleep. I assumed it was safe. Wrong! Another that I simply found strange is that in several scenes, the guard says, "O.K. It's your turn." and then walks away. I didn't realize that one took turns in war. Oh, well . . .

Metal Gear is a game of exploration. Weapons and supplies are hidden in strategic locations. You'll bump into a lot of them inside trucks and behind doors. Others can only be obtained after performing the correct actions. Clues—in the game and on the included play map—will help you, but neither source is completely trustworthy.

Instructions

The manual is well written, thoroughly illustrated, and easy to follow. Too bad the screen captions weren't written by the same person. Metal Gear also includes a detailed map that shows the locations of important objects. There are just enough marked that, if you avoid dying early on, you can make decent progress. It's a nice way to give players a head start.

Features

Metal Gear has exotic military weaponry, passcards to let you through locked doors, and rations to restore your energy. The game offers unlimited Continues, as well as a password option. Each time you use a Continue or password, you retain only your weapons and equipment, not Solid Snake's position in the game.

The direction a guard is facing is not always a good indication of whether he can safely be attacked. Many appear to have the ability to shoot with their backs turned towards you. At times, this makes for extremely frustrating play.

Sound and Graphics

Although the graphics include a fair amount of detail, it's sometimes hard to tell where Solid Snake can or cannot walk. Place his feet a little off the correct path and he can easily die while trying to run away. The graphics are more realistic and detailed inside the buildings than they are in the great outdoors.

The music is standard war-game stuff, but a little more suspenseful than usual. Sound effects—gunshots and the like—are well done.

Challenge

Metal Gear is a tough game, particularly in the beginning. Since you start without weapons or supplies, it will take most players several hours just to reach a point where it's worth saving the game and getting a password. After that, a lot depends on learning the best way to get through each part of Outer Heaven, and what type of attack works best in each situation.

Play Value

Metal Gear has a devoted group of followers. The action is always hot and heavy, and Solid Snake can be killed at almost every turn. Dedicated players who stick with it, though, have a fairly good chance of beating it.

Tips, Tricks, and Strategies

■ Just before you open the first door with Card 1, you'll find a truck that contains rations. You can keep going back in until you have a full set of three rations and have completely restored your life points.

■ Don't believe everything you hear or read. Keys or items shown as needed to open doors aren't always correct. Similarly, trap floors aren't always illustrated on the map. *[GJ]*

■ When you can go no further in building 1, go to the truck on the map marked "Truck for Surrender." *[GJ]*

■ Pick up every hostage Solid Snake finds and be careful not to kill them. If you do, you'll lose a star. And if you want to be able to carry the ammunition you need in some areas, you'll need all the stars you can get. *[GJ]*

■ When a pitfall trap opens up and you go to the Select screen, the trap appears to be closed when you return. It isn't. *[GJ]*

■ To defeat the tank, hide in front of the building, run straight out, drop a mine, and run quickly back. *[GJ]*

■ You can easily defeat the fire trooper if you run above him, and then use the machine gun from one spot. *[GJ]*

■ At higher areas (building 3, for example), some cameras shoot lasers instead of sounding an alert. *[GJ]*

If you've given up on Metal Gear, see "Super Secrets" for more tips.

Mickey Mousecapade

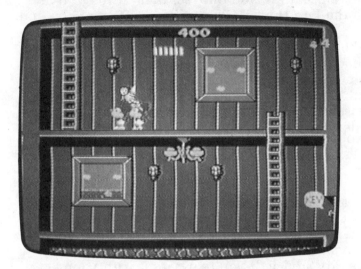

Classification	Kids' Game
Players	1
Controller	Standard
Pause	Yes
Restart at Last Level	Start at any level
Manufacturer	Capcom USA, Inc.
Retail Price	$42.95

Ratings

Instructions	████████░░	6
Features	██████████	10
Graphics	██████████	10
Sound	██████████	10
Challenge	█████████░	7
Play Value	8.45	

Review

Mickey Mousecapade is an arcade game featuring Mickey and Minnie Mouse. In it, you'll direct them through five adventures: the Fun House, Ocean, Woods, Pirate Ship, and Castle.

In the Fun House, the object is to find Mickey and Minnie's shooting stars (so they'll have some protection against the cartoon creatures they meet) and a key that will let them out. In the Woods, you must move them through the four seasons. In the Ocean, Pirate Ship, and Castle, they must defeat a nasty enemy (you'll find the crocodile from Peter Pan and Peg Leg Pete in the first two).

Instructions

For a kids' game, there isn't nearly enough detail provided in the instruction booklet. It tells nothing at all about Mickey's enemies, how to find the Guardian Angel, or what you have to do to get through any stage other than the first one. My advice: If you're a parent with young children, read the manual carefully (followed by this review and the tips below), try out the game, and then explain it to your children.

Features

Mickey Mousecapade starts you off with five lives instead of the usual three. This give kids a better chance of progressing before Mickey and Minnie are lost. If they get bored exploring the Fun House, they can try out any level of the game using a special control pad sequence that's explained in the manual (page 10). Note, however, that even if you complete the level, you'll have to start over at the Fun House when you're through. (It doesn't "count" unless you started from the game's beginning.)

Sound and Graphics

The graphics show great detail, and are perfect for catching kids' attention and keeping them interested. The music and sound effects are appropriate.

Challenge

When they first start playing, most kids will spend a lot of time in the Fun House. Not by choice, however. Until they get magic stars for their characters, it's easy to be defeated. If the crow carries Minnie away, it may be better to restart the game than to go through the headache of finding keys and guessing which statue you must touch to free her.

In other areas (such as the ocean), unless they have a lot of life force left, Mickey and Minnie are frequently lost in the final battle. Once kids have had sufficient practice and learn the little tricks necessary to stay alive, they'll find the play easier and progress much faster.

Play Value

There's a lot of play value in Mickey Mousecapade. Although we've had the game for several months, my youngest son is still trying to beat the Castle. (The fact that he's still interested is a real testimonial for the game.)

Tips, Tricks, and Strategies

- You can shoot from ladders in the Fun House.
- Secret objects are hidden all over. Try shooting everywhere. If Mickey or Minnie's star strikes something, shoot another five or six times in the same spot to uncover a surprise. (This is how to find the Guardian Angels.) [ES]
- Shoot the paintings in the Fun House to find a 1-Up.
- To defeat the magic brooms, you must shoot their handles.
- Not all hidden surprises are pleasant. Sometimes you'll uncover a crow that will kidnap Minnie. To avoid being carried off, shoot from doorways so you can escape quickly if you have to. [ES]
- Search for guardian angels to help you speed untouched through some scenes. Be careful, though. The angel won't protect you from your own clumsiness. You can still fall off ledges and into pits. [ES]
- To move between seasons in the Woods, you have to find the right door. Pick the wrong one and you'll go back to the start. (Note: Some doors are hidden.) [JS]

- In the pirate ship, run past the cutthroat at the bottom. *[JS]*
- Jump onto the ladder to avoid the critter at the top left of the ship. *[JS]*
- Aim high to defeat Peg Leg Pete. (For a fool-proof trick, see "Super Secrets.")
- In the castle, you'll find a 1-Up in the room with the creature dressed in brown. *[JS]*
- If you're having trouble starting at different levels, the correct way to do it is to hold down the control pad with one finger while pressing the Select button with your thumb. While holding these down, hit the Start button with the bottom of your thumb. Works every time.

If you've given up on Mickey Mousecapade, see "Super Secrets" for more tips.

Othello

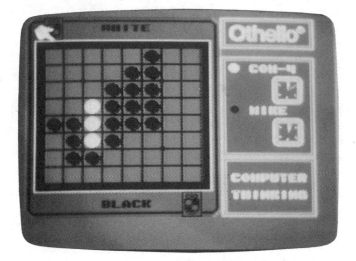

Classification	Misc. (Board Game)
Players	1 or 2
Controller	Standard
Pause	Not applicable
Restart at Last Level	Not applicable
Manufacturer	Acclaim Entertainment
Retail Price	$39.95

Ratings

Instructions	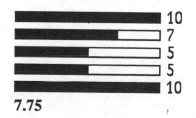	10
Features		7
Graphics		5
Sound		5
Challenge		10
Play Value	7.75	

☐ Othello

Review

Othello is an English board game from the 1800s that became popular in the U.S. in the 1970s. It's played by placing discs (circular tiles) on a grid of 64 squares. Discs are black on one side and white on the other. One side plays black, the other plays white.

At each turn, you place one disc. Each play must trap one or more of your opponent's discs between a pair of yours. Traps can either be vertical, horizontal, diagonal, or a combination of these. After placing your disc, all of your opponent's trapped discs are flipped over to show your color. At the end of the game, the winner is the one with the most discs of his or her color showing.

Instructions

The instructions are excellent and assume you've never heard of Othello before. If you're still not sure how the game is played, you can sit back and watch the Nintendo play demonstration games against itself.

Features

Othello can be played directly against the computer (one-player mode) or against a friend (two-player mode). In the one-player game, there are four skill levels you can choose from. In level 1, you can cancel any move if you change your mind. In levels 2 and 3, the Nintendo takes longer to figure out its moves and you can only cancel three moves during the game. In level 4, no moves can be taken back.

In both one- and two-player games, a time limit can also be set (20, 30, or 40 minutes). If any player takes longer than the limit to make all his or her moves, the game is forfeited. A clock for each player shows the total time taken to that point.

There are several features I've found useful in other computerized versions of Othello that I wish Acclaim had also added. First, the number of counters scored by each side is displayed only at the end of the game. It would have been helpful if a running count were available throughout the game, so you could quickly see how you're doing. Second, particularly for young players, an option to show all legal moves would make it easier for them to pick their moves and help speed up the game. Finally, at the lower levels (say, 1 and 2), another useful feature would be to have the computer suggest your best move. Since it already uses a fairly sophisticated strategy to determine moves, I suspect it wouldn't be too tough to add this option.

Sound and Graphics

Since all play takes place on a green board with black and white discs, there isn't much here to speak of. The graphics used are fine for this game. Same for sound effects. They're simple, but appropriate. The buzz that sounds when you try an illegal move is annoying, though.

Challenge

In one-player mode, Othello is extremely tough to beat. (I was one of the millions of people who bought the board game when it first came out. It still took me over 20 tries to beat the computer at the easiest level!) The "Cancel" feature helps a little, but often not enough. Because it's so hard to win, many players may quickly get discouraged and give up. I'd really like to see level 1 changed to make the computer a little dumber. Everyone needs to see some payoff for their efforts.

Play Value

Othello is a good thinking game for teenagers and adults, but is extremely difficult to beat—even at the easiest levels. You may find it's more fun in two-player mode (no one likes to lose all the time).

Tips, Tricks, and Strategies

- If you're a new Othello player, start by practicing against a friend. Hopefully, he'll be kinder to you than the Nintendo will be.
- The key to winning at Othello lies in capturing and controlling the four corners and, to a smaller degree, the outer edges of the board.
- Try to spread your pieces out rather than clustering them together. Although large blocks of pieces may look great in the beginning, they give your opponent an easy way to control lots of them towards the game's end.

Pac-Man

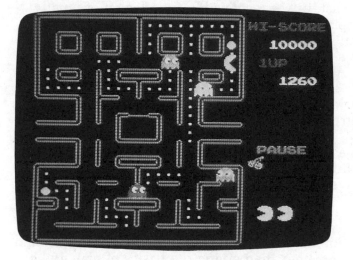

Classification	Arcade
Players	1 or 2
Controller	Standard
Pause	Yes
Restart at Last Level	No
Manufacturer	Tengen
Retail Price	$39.95

Ratings

Instructions	██████████	10
Features	██████░░░░	6
Graphics	███████░░░	7
Sound	█████████░	9
Challenge	█████████░	9
Play Value	8.15	

Note: Although not licensed by Nintendo, Tengen produces games that are compatible with the NES.

Review

Pac-Man was one of the first great arcade games. By itself, it might be considered responsible for creating the industry. At the least, it was responsible for a legion of fanatic players dumping millions of quarters into Pac-Man machines.

Pac-Man is a pie-shaped creature whose mission is to roam about a maze, gobbling up dots, power pellets, fruit, and ghosts. As you clear dots from the maze, a fruit symbol occasionally appears and is worth extra points. If you run over a power pellet, the ghosts that have been chasing Pac-Man will turn blue. As long as they stay blue, they can be eaten, too.

The object of the game is to clear as many screens as possible, while acquiring points. The game ends when all Pac-Men have been caught by the ghosts.

Instructions

The instruction manual is simple and to the point, but then so is the game. Other than giving the basics of play and a few pointers, there's little else that the manual could be expected to offer.

Features

In many respects, Pac-Man is faithful enough to the original arcade version—in features, design, and sound—to bring a nostalgic tear to any older game player's eye. And yet, although it *looks* like the arcade version, the Tengen Pac-Man is missing two design elements that made the original so exciting, challenging, and playable. First, it was popular because of the presence of *patterns*. If you worked hard, you could discover a movement pattern that would carry you safely and successfully through each new level. Learning the Pac-Man patterns was a mark of the true game player. If there are patterns here, they aren't the same as in the arcade version or as readily apparent.

Second, responsiveness to the control pad isn't what it might be. Many times you'll find yourself vainly trying to turn a corner while Pac-Man insists on going straight. It's not clear whether the problem is with the NES' capabilities, the current "state of the art" in NES controller design, or the Pac-Man game itself. Whatever the problem, it makes it a tough game to master—particularly when compared to the arcade version or the many microcomputer releases.

Sound and Graphics

The music is faithful to the arcade game. The graphics, too, although not fancy, mirror those of the original and also include the same cartoon breaks between levels.

Challenge

Several things make Pac-Man tough and challenging. First, the more levels you advance, the faster the ghosts move. Couple this with spotty joystick control and you end up with a game that will leave most players gasping by the time they reach level 4. (Good luck completing that level, by the way.) Although you can gain an additional Pac-Man at 10,000 points, don't look for others; there aren't any.

Play Value

Pac-Man will be of more interest to older players who were around in the early days of the video arcades. Although faithful to the original, it might have been a better idea to jazz it up a bit and bring it into the 1990s. Without an option to restart at the last level, many players will never see level 5. Ms. Pac-Man might have been a better choice for a classic revival. At least the screens change as you advance through the levels.

Tips, Tricks, and Strategies

- If you can, watch the ghosts' eyes. They show the direction they'll move next.
- Whenever possible, take your time. The faster you move, the more likely you'll run right into the ghosts' arms.
- After reaching 10,000 points, concentrate on clearing the boards rather than snaring ghosts. It's the only way you'll ever see the higher levels.

P.O.W.

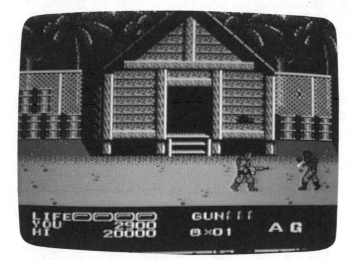

Classification	Arcade
Players	1
Controller	Standard
Pause	Yes
Restart at Last Level	Yes
Manufacturer	SNK Corp. of America
Retail Price	$44.95

Ratings

Instructions	██████████████████	10
Features	████████████████☐	9
Graphics	████████████████☐	9
Sound	██████████████████	10
Challenge	██████████████████	10
Play Value	9.60	

☐ P.O.W.

Review

Your code name is Bart. As a member of the Army Special
Forces, your assignment is to allow yourself to be taken
prisoner by GOON (Government Of Offensive Network).
Once in their P.O.W. camp, you must escape and do whatever you can to break up the international smuggling ring
they've formed. Do it fast before the world economy
collapses!

Bart is uniquely qualified for this mission. He is an expert in hand-to-hand combat and has more than a passing
familiarity with most weapons (which he'll find scattered
throughout the game).

The game is divided into four large areas: the prison
camp, the industrial area, the jungle, and enemy headquar-
ters. In each, you'll find dozens of guards and comman-
dos—some armed, some not. You can borrow the weapons
from some of them if you don't hit them too hard.

P.O.W. has much the same look and feel as Double
Dragon. If you like Double Dragon, you'll like P.O.W., too.

Instructions

The instruction manual is short but effective. Everything
you need to know is discussed. It also includes a detailed
explanation of the power-up items: how each is obtained,
what it's good for, and how long it lasts. There are no
hints, but since high scores depend more on reflexes rather
than strategy, there aren't a lot of hints that could be given.

Features

Bart has four basic moves: punch, kick, jump kick, and
backhand punch. If he can take them away from the enemies, Bart can also acquire weapons, such as a knife, a
machine-gun with ten rounds of ammunition, and hand
grenades. Other weapons and protective devices, such as
brass knuckles and a bullet-proof vest that's also effective
against thrown knives are awarded to Bart after beating
different groups of enemies. An L icon that completely restores his current life can also be won in some areas.

Weapons can be classified in one of two ways: limited
use (knives and hand grenades are good for one toss only,

126

for example) and unlimited use (the brass knuckles and bullet-proof vest are his until the current life is lost). Bart starts each game with three lives. Once all have been lost, you can continue from the beginning of the last level as often as you want.

Sound and Graphics

P.O.W. has outstanding graphics—good background designs and clearly defined characters. You can even see Bart's bulging muscles. As the screen gets crowded with characters, however, there's a lot of flicker to contend with.

The sound quality—both of music and noises—is excellent. It makes the game exciting. The gunshots and explosions are all first-rate.

Challenge

It will take most players several hours to get Bart out of the first level and escape from the P.O.W. camp. Level two is worse. With life power-ups apparently restricted to one per level (frequently in areas where they're not really needed), P.O.W. leaves little room for error. Without at least two full lives, it's very difficult to complete the final encounter in each level.

The unlimited Continues for each area may tempt you to leave the game on for hours at a time, especially if you finally make it to a new level at bedtime. Too bad there isn't a password option.

Play Value

P.O.W. is a carefully engineered program. The graphics and sound are excellent, and the action is fast-paced and exciting. SNK should have a hit on their hands with this one.

Tips, Tricks, and Strategies

■ As soon as you knock a soldier down, move in close and hit or kick him again as soon as he tries to rise. (No points here for being a nice guy and fighting fair.)

☐ P.O.W.

- Be careful not to get too close to your enemies. If you move too far forward, your kicks and punches won't connect. And it's easy to get hit as you move through the soldier or back off.
- In level 1, kick or hit the soldier carrying the machine gun to make him drop it. If you throw a knife at him, he falls off the screen, taking the gun with him. Also, if you even attack the soldier to your left (the one with the knife) before going after the machine-gunner, the gun disappears when the soldier carrying it is dispatched.
- Move into sheds, barracks, and trucks as quickly as you can. In many cases, this will keep you from having to fight the soldiers outside of it twice—once going in and once going out.
- You can go back into enclosures that contain power-ups if they haven't scrolled off screen. This is a handy trick if you lose your powers when you step outside (because Bart bought the farm).
- You can use a jump kick to knock riders off their motor-cycles. Be sure to move out of the way quickly to avoid being blown up when the motorcycle explodes, though.
- When you're in the tunnel in level 2, it's best to avoid the motorcycles entirely. Stay against the lower wall and walk out quickly. Then move to the spot closest to the front of the screen at the tunnel's end. The cyclist will pass right by you.
- In level 2, several Green Berets jump down from towers. Right after the first one lands, move back to the left to fight him. This will keep more from coming. Keep using this trick and you can tackle them one at a time, instead of three at once.
- When battling the frogmen in level 2, watch for their tell-tale splashes and you can surprise them when they pop up.
- Keep an eye on your score. You're awarded an extra life at every multiple of 30,000 points.
- You move between levels with only the lives you have left. Don't be afraid of losing Bart if you don't have many life points. When you Continue from the level, they'll be completely restored.

R.C. Pro-AM

Classification	Arcade
Players	1
Controller	Standard
Pause	Yes
Restart at Last Level	Yes
Manufacturer	Nintendo of America, Inc.
Retail Price	$34.95

Ratings

Instructions	██████████████	10
Features	█████████████▢	9
Graphics	████████████▢▢	8
Sound	██████████████	10
Challenge	█████████████▢	9
Play Value	9.20	

Review

If you're into driving games, Nintendo released this classic that you're sure to enjoy. R.C. Pro-AM lets you control a tiny radio-controlled car, steering it around a variety of treacherous race courses. To make things interesting, each course has hazards such as puddles, rain squalls, oil slicks, and pop-up barriers. As you speed around the track to the tune of squealing tires and racing engines, you can collect items that increase your power (turbo accelerator and a hotter engine) and your adhesion to the track (sticky tires).

In each race, it's you against three drone cars for a specified number of laps. As long as you beat at least one of them, you'll advance to the next course. Between races you'll be shown a display of the power-ups that are currently in effect, the track condition, and the number of laps for the next race.

Instructions

The instruction manual is well written and tells you what you need to know. Most of the illustrations of game items are hand-drawn, but are close enough to what the objects look like on screen to avoid any confusion.

Features

There's more than just racing to this game. Since the drone cars tend to recover quickly and make fewer mistakes than most humans will, Nintendo has given you one advantage that they don't have—weapons. You can collect missiles and bombs to take care of your opponents for those rare moments when racing skill alone won't quite do. Also, if you hit enough bonus letters to spell NINTENDO, you'll be awarded a higher-class car.

Progress around the track is shown as a closeup of your car and also as a tiny inset on the screen. Your dot is the red one.

Each time you place first, second, or third, you get another gold, silver, or bronze addition to your trophy case. R.C. Pro-AM allows you two Continues after placing in the first race. Just like the arcade machines, at the end of the game you have ten seconds to press the Start button if you want to continue. High scores—if they're high enough—are registered on a champion's screen at the end of the game.

Sound and Graphics

The sound effects in R.C. Pro-AM are great. The squealing of hot tires as you swerve around corners and the explosions when a car crashes or is blown up are perfect. The graphics are okay, but not as exciting. Everything is easily recognizable.

Challenge

The challenge of R.C. Pro-AM is mostly one of reflexes and coordination, rather than strategy. If you can move the car smoothly through turns, hit the power-up and weapon objects, use your weapons effectively, and recover quickly from crashes, you'll do well.

Play Value

You'll get a lot of play out of R.C. Pro-AM. It takes a master driver and a great deal of practice to reach the upper race limit—here are 32 different ones.

Tips, Tricks, and Strategies

■ Save your weapons for when they're really needed. Pulling a last-minute third out of a defeat is one example of a good use. Keep in mind that weapons won't be found in all races, but your existing stash will carry over from one race to the next.
■ You can only have one weapon at a time. If you prefer the rocket over the bomb, for instance, swapping weapons is just a matter of running over the one you want.

- Pick up all roll cages you see. It's the only item the drones will grab if you don't.
- Move to the center of the track on straightaways. If your car brushes against the sides, it will slow down.
- Try not to miss any of the bonus letters. The faster you spell *NINTENDO*, the quicker you can upgrade to a faster car.
- Stay to the edges in the seventh race to avoid crashing into the pop-up barriers.

RoboWarrior

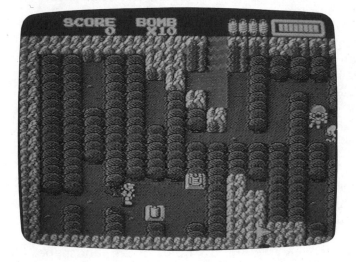

Classification	Arcade
Players	1
Controller	Standard
Pause	Yes
Restart at Last Level	Yes
Manufacturer	Jaleco USA, Inc.
Retail Price	$39.95

Ratings

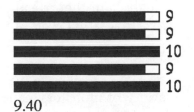

Instructions		9
Features		9
Graphics		10
Sound		9
Challenge		10
Play Value	9.40	

Review

Some time in the future, overpopulation and pollution
have made the Earth virtually uninhabitable. In an effort to
save the people, a great scientist named Altile orders the
construction of an artificial planet and ships a portion of
the Earth's population there.

Two thousand years later, the beautiful planet Altile
(named after its creator) is attacked and overrun by invaders from the Xantho Empire. The inhabitants flee underground. In an effort to save Altile and defeat the invaders,
Earth sends the most powerful of its robots, the Z-type
Earth Defense cyborg—ZED, for short. RoboWarrior is the
story of Zed's attempt to recapture the planet and defeat
the hideous invaders that now occupy it.

RoboWarrior is a game of exploration. Although Zed
starts with only a laser pistol and a handful of bombs,
many powerful items have been hidden by the people to
aid him in his quest. To uncover them, he must use his
bombs and other weapons to blow holes in the landscape.
And blowing things up is a large part of RoboWarrior's fun!

Instructions

Unlike many games where it's obvious that a story line
was hastily tacked on at the end, RoboWarrior's plot reads
like good science fiction. The instructions are beautifully
illustrated in full color and include many sample screen
shots from the game.

The manual's only shortcoming is that the illustrations
of the power objects and treasures—while beautiful—are
different enough from their display on screen to sometimes
leave you guessing. Otherwise, it's a model instruction
booklet.

Features

The huge variety of monsters—each with its own attack
characteristic—and the number of super powers that can
be found are unusual for an arcade game. Because of the
length of time it takes to complete RoboWarrior, however,
it really could use a Save Game or password option. Once
you've turned off the NES, you'll have to start over from

the beginning. Also, much of the fun is in exploring all the nooks and crannies of each level. It would be nice if backwards scrolling were possible.

Sound and Graphics

The graphics are state-of-the-art. Even when you blow things up, they don't just go poof and disappear. Depending on a bomb's placement, more or less of the tree or rock it is set next to will explode or shatter.

RoboWarrior's sound effects are snappy. I was particularly impressed by the echo effect used for bomb blasts. When Zed is destroyed, the sound is very similar to what you'd hear if you were about to pass out. Interesting . . . The theme music is fast-moving and matches the game's pace, but since it never changes (except when the game is over), it gets boring quickly.

Challenge

Although an arcade game, it takes strategy to advance through the levels. If you don't have a sufficient stock of certain devices, such as life vests, lanterns, and candles, or can't find them within the level, even the unlimited Continues won't be of much help. You must plan ahead.

Play Value

RoboWarrior is a super role-playing game; one of the best of its kind. Just blowing things up to see if anything is hidden underneath is fun. Once you've added in the search for hidden keys and chalices, the accumulation of weapons and special devices, and the strategy needed to complete each level and defeat the evil lords, you have one great game!

Tips, Tricks, and Strategies

■ When you destroy an enemy, a single blue bomb will be left behind. If you don't pick it up quickly, it will disappear. On the other hand, special powers you uncover will wait for you to collect them. Don't pick up life pods until you really need them. (On the other hand, make sure they don't scroll off-screen without collecting them!)

- Even though candles may be sufficient for exploring underground areas, lamps make things a lot easier. Stock up on them when Zed visits the store. (Buy at least one in the first store you see.)

- If you're stuck underground without a candle, don't give up. Unless you're very low on energy, you can often bump into the exit if you use a little strategy while exploring blind.

- Stuck inside or outside a walled area? Sometimes it takes several bombs to blow a hole in a wall.

- Chalices and keys are frequently hidden within hard-to-reach places. Don't always take the easiest path.

- Keep one eye on Zed's energy level. By the time you hear the warning beeps, it's often too late. If you have a willing friend, ask him or her to be a "spotter" for you.

- Don't wait until the last second to restore Zed's energy. If he gets hit by some of the invaders (like the Lurcher robots), Zed can easily be destroyed before you can do anything about it. You should restore any time energy drops below one—but, preferably, a little before then.

- If you're about to run out of energy, try taking a quick trip underground. If you're lucky, you may find an energy capsule before you pass away. Also, don't waste special powers simply because you're dying. It's better to have them around in the next game. (Note, however, that Zed loses half his powers each time you Continue.)

- You can find the key for Period 2-1 along the upper wall, next to an entrance to the underground.

- It's critical to possess certain items if you want to complete some levels. For Periods 2-2 and 3-2, you'll need plenty of candles or a lantern. Life vests are often crucial, but there's usually several of them scattered around. Plan ahead unless you'd like to be stuck in some periods indefinitely.

- Don't stroll into the waterfalls, even with a life vest. On the other hand, you can safely walk across any single square of water if you move fast.

- If some areas seem to go on forever, it's because you haven't found the key and, in some cases, the chalice. Try exploring different areas. Assuming you live long enough to find what you're looking for, you can still get out.
- Globula, the first Xantho Lord, can be taken out with bombs. (Use the special boots if you get hit too easily.)
- Zed's defensive power increases with score. According to Jaleco, you'll notice an increase at each of the following point levels: 80000, 180000, 300000, 500000, 800000, 1000000, and 1200000.

If you've given up on RoboWarrior, see "Super Secrets" for more tips.

Sesame Street 1 2 3

Classification	Kids' Game (Educational)
Players	1
Controller	Standard
Pause	No
Restart at Last Level	No
Manufacturer	Hi Tech Expressions
Retail Price	$34.95

Ratings

Instructions		10
Features		9
Graphics		10
Sound		9
Challenge		7
Play Value	8.95	

Review

If you're still wondering if there's any educational material for the Nintendo, wonder no longer. It's Sesame Street to the rescue! Hi Tech Expressions has produced a cartridge that teaches shape, color, and pattern recognition (Ernie's Magic Shapes), and counting, addition, and subtraction (Astro-Grover).

There are 11 variations of the games—six for Ernie's Magic Shapes and five for Astro-Grover. Each lesson is a gentle introduction to a useful skill area without the typical razzes or buzzers that often greet incorrect answers in other children's computer programs.

Lessons progress in difficulty. Astro-Grover has an outer space theme, and starts with two counting games. In the first (Count the Zips), a space ship beams between one and nine spacemen onto the screen and the child indicates the number shown by selecting it with the control pad. If two mistakes are made in a row, Grover pops his head up to show the right answer. For each correct answer, a part of a city is beamed down. Five right answers finish the construction of the city and the game.

The second counting game (Beam That Number) is more difficult. It starts with a screenful of Zips, and a beam is shined on some of them. If the number of highlighted Zips matches the number shown on the spaceship, and the child must press the A or B button. If it's the wrong number, the child presses the control pad and the beam will highlight a new set of Zips.

Lessons three and four use the Zips to teach elementary addition and subtraction skills. In the final lesson (Sum Up, Sum Down), the child must select the right combination of one, two, or three numbers that equals the number on the spaceship.

Ernie's Magic Shapes has Ernie performing a magic show with a magic wand, top hat, and a bunny. A shape is shown above his head. When one that matches in color, size, and shape appears above the hat, the child selects it by pressing the A or B button. If it's not the right one, the child indicates this by pressing the control pad. If correct, Ernie waves his magic wand, the shape is floated to the top of the screen, and the bunny applauds. If the child is wrong, the bunny pops out and momentarily shakes its head.

As in Astro-Grover, Ernie's Magic Shape games progress in difficulty. They begin with simple shape recognition, move to shape and color matching, and finally to identifying embedded shapes within figures. An example of the latter might require choosing the triangles, rectangles, and circles that a rocket ship is composed of. There is no penalty for skipping past a shape that's correct. It will eventually show up again, so the child can choose it later.

Instructions
The instructions are intended for adults, since the children are not expected to be able to read. They are clearly written and offer useful suggestions for how parents can take part in the games.

Features
Controls have deliberately been kept simple. In general, the child must either pick a number from the screen (Astro-Grover), or press a button to accept a shape or the control pad to reject one. When the child wants to change lessons, he or she has only to press Select or Start and a menu for the current game appears. Unfortunately, the control pad cannot be used to change between Astro-Grover and Ernie's Magic Shapes. To do this, the program must be restarted by pressing the NES' reset button.

Sound and Graphics
Cute music, but it never varies from its few simple themes. On the other hand, your child will always know when he or she has gotten something right, since the same music always accompanies a correct answer.

Challenge
Ernie's Magic Shapes is designed for preschoolers. Although not stated, I suspect that the numerical problems in Astro-Grover would be suitable for ages 5 through 7.

Play Value

Astro-Grover provides an excellent visual approach to math using a subject matter that most children can relate to. Once a child has learned to count, Astro-Grover seems a to be good way to introduce mathematical concepts without the stress that might accompany classroom instruction.

Similarly, Ernie's Magic Shapes does a good job of teaching shape, color, and pattern identification while having some fun in the process. My kids enjoy both games and have continued to play them even though they've been mastered.

Super Mario Bros.

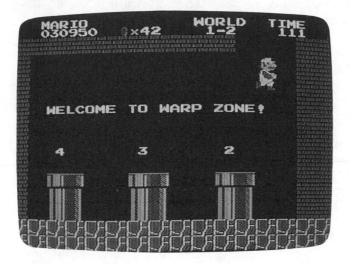

Classification	Arcade
Players	1 or 2
Controller	Standard
Pause	Yes
Restart at Last Level	Yes (see text)
Manufacturer	Nintendo of America, Inc.
Retail Price	$24.95

Ratings

Instructions		8
Features		10
Graphics		9
Sound		10
Challenge		10
Play Value	9.45	

Review

The once-peaceful Mushroom Kingdom has fallen on hard times. Its people have been bewitched by the Koopa, an invading horde of evil turtles, and have been turned into bricks, stones, and plants. Princess Toadstool, the only one who can restore the kingdom, is being held captive by the Koopa King. Mario and his brother Luigi are the kingdom's last hope for the princess' rescue.

Features

The Mushroom Kingdom is split into eight worlds, each with four levels. In your normal guise, there's little you can do except run and jump quickly to avoid the Koopa and, occasionally, stomp on some of them. However, in many of the levels, the Mushroom people have hidden secret powers to help you battle the Koopa. They can make you temporarily invincible (Starman), give you an additional life (1-UP Mushroom), change you into a giant-sized Super Mario (Magic Mushroom), or give you magic fireballs (Fire Flower).

Super Mario Bros. is packed with hidden objects. A big part of the game's fun is in finding their locations. (Do you know where all the hidden coin boxes and 1-UP Mushrooms are?)

Other than Bowser, King of the Koopa, most of the enemies you'll run into are sort of cute. Even young kids, if they can handle arcade action, will enjoy this one.

Sound and Graphics

The Super Mario Bros. theme music is known by almost as many people as the Pac-Man theme. The graphics, although very well done, don't show quite the attention to fine detail that some others do.

Challenge

One thing that makes this such a superb game is that, although it's difficult to advance, you'll improve with practice. If you get stuck on some of the lower levels, you can skip past them by using the Warp Zones. Working for a high score almost seems secondary to finding the hidden objects.

Play Value

Super Mario Bros. is the game that all others will be judged by. Its superb combination of challenge, features, graphics, and music makes it a game to be played over and over. There are so many mysteries to uncover and tricks to master, that it will keep players coming back for a long time. There's always something new to discover.

Even knowing the secret tricks and the locations of special objects, it will take you a *long* time to rescue the princess and complete World 8. There are many obstacles that, at times, will have you muttering under your breath as you struggle to learn the maneuvers that will let you proceed. Practice and the willingness to explore, however, are always rewarded.

In addition to the tips below, check out the diagram in this chapter for additional hints concerning the whereabouts of some important objects. It won't tell you *exactly* where things are hidden—just the World each one is in. (Hey, finding the stuff is the fun part!)

Tips, Tricks, and Strategies

■ Tired of starting over from scratch each time Mario runs out of lives? To restart from the last world you were in, just hold down the A button and then press Start when you see the screen that asks you to select the number of players. This will continue to work until the unit is turned off.

Failure to include this in the manual cost Super Mario Bros. one rating point. For some players, this single piece of information may mean the difference between shelving the game and coming back for more.

■ Good things lie above. You'll find invisible coins and mushrooms by simply jumping straight up in the right spots. Some of the mushrooms (the 1-UP variety) will give you an extra life. The first one is hidden halfway through World 1-1.

☐ Super Mario Bros.

- Try squatting on top of each drain pipe. Some of them lead to interesting shortcuts or ways to get additional powers and coins.
- Master the running jump (jumping while holding down the B button). At the end of each level, if you use this jump from a high vantage point, you can ride the flag down to the bottom for 5,000 points! Without the running jump, you'll find that it's impossible to complete some levels [ES].
- Some bricks conceal multiple coins. The faster you punch, the more coins you'll receive.
- If you've a rapid fire switch on your controller, set button B to the highest level. It doesn't gain you a lot, but it's really interesting when used to throw fireballs! (This only works with controllers that have a separate rapid-fire switch for each button. If button A is also set for rapid-fire, you'll find that Mario can't jump correctly.)
- In World 1-2, there's a floating shelf with a line of coins suspended above it. Move to the far right edge of the shelf and punch the ceiling. You'll reveal a 1-UP mushroom. Now quickly punch the brick to its right to make a hole and jump to the ground. The mushroom is yours.
- After you've gained experience and have tried the first three worlds, it's time to search for the Warp Zones. (A Warp Zone lets you jump from the present level directly to another higher-level world.) The first one can be found in World 1-2 if you move Mario to an "unusual" spot; this is somewhere where you normally wouldn't think of going. If you really hunt, there's one in World 4-2 that will take you into World 6, 7, or—ta-da—8. If you don't find this Warp Zone, there's an easy one to find in this same level that will take you to World 5.
- At the beginning of World 4-1, you'll meet up with Lakitu and his never-ending supply of Spiny eggs. The Spinys that hatch can be destroyed with fireballs. If you don't have fireballs, you can stop Lakitu from making eggs by climbing onto the highest brick and jumping onto its head.
- Without fireballs, you'll have a tough time getting past the Hammer Brothers (hammer-throwing turtle buddies). If possible, try bumping them off their bricks from beneath. Another tactic that frequently works is to run as

fast as you can until you're out of range of their hammers.

■ If you're tired of being fried or stomped by Bowser, King of the Koopa (turtle dragon), try running under him while in Super Mario form. If you get stomped, you'll be invincible for a few seconds, which is more than enough time to get past him. If he misses you, all the better. Either way, you win. Other approaches that also work include throwing fireballs and riding the platform overhead until you're safely past.

■ Rescuing the princess isn't all there is to Super Mario Bros. There is life after World 8 *[JH]*.

If you've given up on Super Mario Bros., see "Super Secrets" for more tips.

Super Mario Bros. Highlights

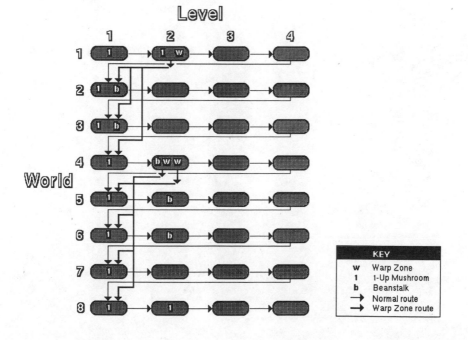

Super Mario Bros. 2

Classification	Arcade
Players	1
Controller	Standard
Pause	Yes
Restart at Last Level	Yes
Manufacturer	Nintendo of America, Inc.
Retail Price	$39.95

Ratings

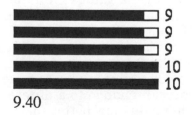

Instructions	9
Features	9
Graphics	9
Sound	10
Challenge	10
Play Value	9.40

Review

In Super Mario Bros. 2, the second saga of Mario, Luigi, and friends, it's their task to free Subcon (the land of dreams) from Wart's curse. Wart is manufacturing evil creatures and guardian monsters using a special dream machine. The monsters range from the innocuous (Shyguys, Hoopsters, and Ninjis) to the insidious (Autobombs, fire-breathing Fryguys, and the powerful three-headed Tryclyde).

Mario's mission is to make his way through the seven Worlds of Subcon (a total of 20 levels) and defeat Wart, if he can. Just living to see all the levels is something few gamers can boast about.

Instructions

The game comes with a good instruction manual, heavily populated with screen shots and drawings. It contains neither playing hints nor any mention of the Warp Zones, however.

Features

There are many differences between features in the two Super Mario games. Super Mario Bros. 2 is a one-player game. This was a good decision, since—as you become a more experienced player—the wait between turns would be much too long if two were playing. Gone are Mario's fireballs. In their place, Mario and friends can throw the vegetables they find growing in Subcon. Starman, however, is still around. Finally, play is no longer for points. The only object of the game is to remain alive and beat Wart.

A welcome new feature is the opportunity to be any of four different characters: Mario, Luigi, Toad, or the Princess. Each has its own jumping, running, and lifting characteristics. The Princess, for instance, has the ability to float in midair for a short time. Any time a new World is entered, you can change to a different character, if you like. (Some characters are better than others, depending on the particular World you're entering.)

Sound and Graphics

The sound effects and music are very good and appropriate to the game. The graphics, especially those that are above ground, are uncluttered and, frankly, a bit sparse. There's not much to look at and certainly nothing to make you go, "Oh, wow!" The detail is much better and usually more interesting below ground.

Challenge

For several reasons, Super Mario Bros. 2 is an exceptionally challenging game. First, unlike the last version, you can only continue twice before being forced to start over from World 1-1. Second, because some of the characters move virtually in slow motion (Luigi's jumps, for instance), it's tough to always make the characters do what you want them to do. Finally, the game requires more wits and strategy than the original did. Quick reflexes aren't enough to get you past several obstacles. There's often only one way past, and you'll have to figure it out for yourself.

Like the original, Super Mario Bros. 2 has secret shortcuts and tricks for you to uncover. This is what adds much of the excitement to the game and accounts for the enthusiasm with which it has been received.

Play Value

With only two Continues, you'll find it necessary to start Super Mario Bros. 2 over from the beginning many times. The opportunity to earn extra lives with the slot machine, however, helps a little. (On the other hand, if you know the secret of how to beat it, the slot machine can help a lot! See Super Secrets for the trick.)

In early attempts at the game, many players will be left in the dust. Without clues, progress may be too slow to satisfy some players. With clues, Super Mario Bros. 2 becomes a more reasonable and rewarding challenge.

Tips, Tricks, and Strategies

■ Where you throw the vials of magic potion is extremely important. Try to surround yourself with grass or cherries when you toss a vial.

151

- Having trouble jumping far enough? Run and hold down button B as you jump.
- Watch for shortcuts. In World 1-1, for instance, you may have wondered if there's anything on the other side of the waterfall. Try it with a good jumper and see what happens.
- Be careful in Sub-space. You can lose lives there, too.
- Phanto will stop chasing you if you drop his key. It makes a great weapon, by the way.
- Don't get carried away with knocking off the creatures of Subcon. Since you aren't playing for points, leave them alone if they aren't a threat to you.
- Getting three of a kind on the slot machine isn't all luck. It's a matter of timing. Try pausing exactly the same amount between each button click. Once you get the rhythm right, it gets easier.
- To beat some of the bosses, you must find a way to use their weapons against them.
- You'll be happy to learn that Super Mario Bros. 2 also has its share of Warp Zones. You can find one leading from World 1-3 to World 4-1 if you enter Sub-space in a special spot.
- Jump over the Ostro at the end of World 2-1 to give yourself some egg-catching room.
- In World 2-2, you can use the mushroom blocks to defeat the Ostro. You'll need a strong jumper like Luigi to get to him, though.
- The Princess' jumping and floating skills come in handy on the ice in World 4.
- Even though they look solid, characters can jump up through the ice blocks.
- In World 4-2, it's okay to land on top of the whale's water spout, but not to run into it. You can also land safely on a whale's tale if you jump carefully.
- In World 6-1, go down the jar with the mushroom on it for 1-Ups.
- Most creatures you meet can be jumped on and tossed. Don't forget it! (It's fun to throw Cobrats.)
- If you enter Sub-space more than twice in the same level, you'll pick vegetables instead of coins. *[GJ]*

If you've given up on Super Mario Bros. 2, see "Super Secrets" for more tips.

Taboo the Sixth Sense

Classification	Misc. (Adult Cartridge)
Players	1
Controller	Standard
Pause	No
Restart at Last Level	No
Manufacturer	Tradewest, Inc.
Retail Price	$39.95

Ratings

Instructions	████████████████	9
Features	████████████████	8
Graphics	████████████████	9
Sound	████████████████	9
Challenge	Not applicable	
Play Value	8.69	

Review

Taboo the Sixth Sense is a different type of program for the NES. (Note that I said *program*, not game.) It's a personal fortune teller. Each time you plug the cartridge in, Taboo uses tarot cards to divine the answers to questions you have about the future.

A tarot deck consists of 78 ancient cards, divided—like our playing cards—into four suits: wands, cups, swords, and coins. Twenty-two of them are referred to as Trump cards. Each card in the deck has its own meaning. Once a question has been asked, the cards are shuffled and ten are dealt into a Celtic cross arrangement that, when properly interpreted, can give a suggestion of what the future will bring. Like the individual cards, each position in the tableau also has a special meaning. Where the cards are placed is as important as *which* cards are drawn.

To use Taboo, start by answering a few simple questions: name, birth date, and sex. After asking a question about some event in the near future (by selecting the appropriate letters from the display), the cards are shuffled, dealt, and then presented to you one at a time, along with appropriate interpretations for each one.

After the tarot reading has ended, you can try the second part of the program. Taboo will select between one and eight lucky numbers for you. You can specify how many numbers are to be drawn, the minimum and maximum for the group (anywhere between 0 and 99), and what state you're in. Just the thing for lottery players and numerology fans!

Instructions

The instructions do a good job of explaining the history of the tarot and how the divination system works. No, you won't be an expert, but you will know enough about the tarot to use the program effectively.

Features

One feature that could easily have been added is an opening menu that would allow you to choose either the tarot or lucky numbers. As it is, you can't get to the numbers without first completing a tarot reading. Similarly, you can't ask two tarot questions in a row without drawing some numbers in between. It's a minor quibble, but probably reasonable considering how the cartridge will frequently be used; that is, at a party where a bunch of people want to ask questions.

I also wish Taboo had the ability to draw three- and four-digit numbers, instead of just two-digit ones. If it's to be used with a state or local lottery, some people might want to use it to pick the daily number, too. (Of course, if you need a four-digit number, you can always have Taboo pick two two-digit ones and then put them together. Hey, use your imagination.)

Taboo also includes a nice fold-out chart that shows each card of the tarot, along with a brief description of the card's meaning.

Sound and Graphics

The graphics are well done. The constant black background gives the program an air of mystery, which, of course, is perfectly appropriate.

The theme music also fits the program. There are only a few sound effects, which are used for some of the more important Trump cards.

Play Value

Unless you're heavily into the Tarot or the lottery, Taboo will probably be seen as a novelty item for the NES. It's definitely the sort of cartridge you can pull out at parties and use to amuse your friends. Whether it has any real staying power or will just end up on your shelf depends on you.

According to the instructions, Taboo should not be played or sold to anyone under 14 years old. This is a good idea for two reasons. First, young children might have a tendency to rely too heavily on Taboo's interpretations. Since the tarot's answers, like those of many other fortune-telling systems, are purposely vague (it doesn't answer simply yes and no), children might easily be confused by it. Second, anyone under that age is not likely to be interested in the topic, anyway.

Teenage Mutant Ninja Turtles

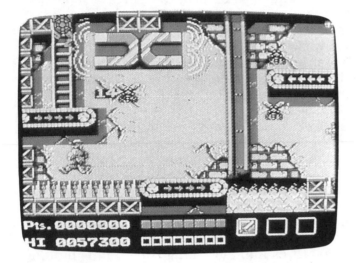

Classification	Arcade
Players	1
Controller	Standard
Pause	Yes
Restart at Last Level	Yes, twice
Manufacturer	Ultra Software Corp.
Retail Price	$43.95

Ratings

Instructions	▬▬▬▬▬▭	7
Features	▬▬▬▬▬▬	10
Graphics	▬▬▬▬▬▬	10
Sound	▬▬▬▬▬▬	10
Challenge	▬▬▬▬▬▬	10
Play Value	9.40	

157

Review

Teenage Mutant Ninja Turtles is a two-part adventure. First, Shredder has kidnapped April, the Turtles' reporter friend. Helpless thing that she is, April must be rescued. That's the easy part. The hard part is making it through the remaining four game levels (each has several stages), confronting Shredder, and capturing his Life Transformer Gun—the only device capable of turning the Turtles' mentor Splinter back into a man. (An unfortunate accident changed him into a rat.)

Confused? Well, if you've never seen the cartoon show, you should be. The Teenage Mutant Ninja Turtles are four oversized turtles that walk on their hind legs, talk, and are masters of the martial arts. Each has a weapon with which he excels: Leonardo uses the Katana Blade, Raphael has his Sai, Michaelangelo uses Nunchukus, and Donatello the Bo. They all have an inordinate fondness for pizza. Shredder is their nemesis, and has transformed many normal creatures into evil beings that do his bidding. Although vicious, most aren't particularly bright. (Their intelligence plays an important role in the television show, but doesn't come into play in the game.)

All four Turtles are yours to command—one at a time. Whenever one is losing strength, you can pop out to the Select screen and swap in one of his buddies. The combat will pick up where it left off. Pizza will restore their life force. When all four Turtles expire, the game ends.

Instructions

The manual explains the plot, how to use the controller and read the Select screen maps, and shows many of the enemies and their point values. Although it's written in good comic-book style and is thoroughly entertaining, more emphasis on the basics is needed.

For instance, the manual states that you can rescue your captured buddies by simply finding and touching them. If they're anywhere in levels 1 or 2, I never bumped into them. It would have helped if the instructions had been more specific on this point. Similarly, additional discussion of jumping techniques, enemy weaknesses, and playing strategies is warranted.

Features

Each Turtle has his different strengths, so they're not inter-changeable. Some of their weapons, for example, are better than others. This means a little strategy will help when confronting particular creatures.

In most scenes, there are three play areas available. There is "outside," where the Turtles are displayed as tiny miniatures and make large movements—between buildings or sewer entrances, for example. There is "inside," where they are shown full-size and do the bulk of their exploring and fighting. Finally, there is the "map view" or Select screen, where an overview of the current area can be found. The maps show the Turtles' current position and places they can enter. Their friends offer helpful clues and encouragement here.

In addition to each Turtle's special weapon (which cannot be lost), a limited number of other powerful weapons can be won in combat. Shurikens and boomerangs are examples of these.

If you lose all the Turtles, you can Continue the game twice from the most recent level. After that, you'll have to start from the beginning.

Sound and Graphics

Super-exciting music and good sound effects. The graphics show an abundance of detail, and the realistic size of the enemies makes them easy to identify and fun to fight. The animation is superb. I was especially impressed by the Tur-tles' tumbling leaps and the way their weapons spin around.

Challenge

Teenage Mutant Ninja Turtles is one tough arcade game! Although level 1 is easy to beat, anything beyond is a mat-ter of timing and luck. It took several days to complete the river sequence and get a glimpse of the third level. Strategy plays only a minor role in the game. It's reflexes all the way.

Play Value

Teenage Mutant Ninja Turtles is one of the new arcade games that exemplifies the best for the NES. Top-notch graphics, sound, and fierce action combine for superb play value. And it's hard enough to keep even the best players occupied for a long time.

Tips, Tricks, and Strategies

- In the sewers, run Rocksteady into the far right wall. He can't turn around, and can be attacked from behind.
- Some areas have pizza at the very end or beginning. Go in and out repeatedly with each Turtle to completely restore their lives.
- You don't have to go into every area in the sewers.
- Use Donatello's Bo to dispatch the Searchlight Mechanisms with one strike. Other weapons often take several hits.
- Be careful on ladders. Turtles are defenseless while climbing.
- Don't just stand there when a creature with a weapon attacks. If you use your weapon at the same time, you can avoid damage.
- The sleeping soldiers are easy to defeat. If you stand just the right distance away from them, you can strike them each time they awaken without getting hit yourself.
- In the river, there's an area of dense seaweed that you must pass through.
- Switch characters in the river before the current one dies. If you don't, you'll have to start the scene over again. Similarly, when time is running out, switch to a character whose life is almost gone. Why waste one with full life?

If you've given up on Teenage Mutant Ninja Turtles, see "Super Secrets" for more tips.

Tetris

Classification	Arcade
Players	1 or 2 simultaneous
Controller	Standard
Pause	Yes
Restart at Last Level	No
Manufacturer	Tengen
Retail Price	$39.95

Ratings

Instructions	████████████▭	9
Features	█████████████	10
Graphics	█████████████	10
Sound	█████████████	10
Challenge	████████████▭	9
Play Value	9.55	

Note: Although not licensed by Nintendo, Tengen produces games that are compatible with the NES.

Review

Even if you've never seen it on the Nintendo, the computer magazines have been making a fuss about Tetris for a long time. And it's well deserved. Tetris is one of the few arcade games around that will exercise your mind as much as your fingers.

It works like this. Puzzle shapes fall from the top of the screen. As they fall, you can move them left or right, and rotate them clockwise or counter-clockwise. The object is to make the puzzle pieces fit into the ones that have already fallen. Each time one or more horizontal rows are completely filled with pieces, those rows are removed from the screen. The more rows you can remove, the longer the game will last. It ends when pieces are stacked all the way to the top of the screen.

Instructions

It's easier to show how Tetris works than to tell how it works. Nevertheless, the manual takes an admirable stab at it. It would have been helpful, however, if more of the play options had been illustrated with screen shots.

If after reading the instructions you still don't get it, watch the NES play a demo game or two. Then try the various play options. You'll quickly catch on.

Features

Tengen has done an admirable job of adding features to Tetris. All play is done on a split screen. In one-player mode, only the left half is used. In two-player mode or play against the computer, both sides are used at the same time. There are also two "cooperative" modes: one where both players receive the same shapes at the same time, and one where the computer attempts to help you.

Whenever a new level is reached, bonuses are awarded for every single, double, triple, and quadruple set of rows cleared. (The latter, by the way, is referred to as a "Tetris.") For your amusement, tiny Russian dancers also go through their dance and acrobatic routines. I love the bow that each takes at the end!

Although there are 18 difficulty levels, you can start at any of the first 9. If things get too easy for you, you can also play with a handicap, where the game is started with 3, 6, 9, or 12 partially filled rows already on the screen. Of course, the higher the level, the faster the shapes fall. After losing, you can restart your side of the game by pressing both the A and B buttons. Tetris will automatically begin at the level you initially selected with the same pieces and handicap.

Sound and Graphics

At last someone is offering a choice of music. At the start of each game, you can select any of four different Russian musical selections to play in the background. If you've had enough noise for the day or someone in the house needs their rest, you can also select "Silence."

Although we're talking mainly about puzzle shapes, the graphics are colorful and beautifully textured.

Challenge

It's pretty easy to move through the first several levels. Success in the higher levels (at their faster speed), on the other hand, will come more slowly. It takes a good eye to determine whether a piece, once rotated, is going to fit correctly into that open slot or not. Single mistakes are seldom fatal, but they can easily lead to a botched game if you let your guard slip.

Play Value

Tetris requires quick wits and nimble fingers if you want to score high. It's sure to be a favorite of teens and adults. Beware, though. Tetris is extremely habit forming!

Tips, Tricks, and Strategies

- Watch the next piece that's waiting to fall while you work on the current one. This will let you make room for it, if it's a special shape.
- Try not to leave tall open slots. They're difficult to fill, and you can't always afford to wait for a long red piece.

- Remember that the long red pieces can also be laid sideways.
- Until your playing skills are finely honed, don't worry about score. Instead, concentrate on advancing through the levels. After you've mastered the basic moves, it's time to learn how to set up doubles, triples, and Tetrises.

The Three Stooges

Classification	Activision, Inc.
Players	1 or 2
Controller	Standard
Pause	Yes
Restart at Last Level	No
Manufacturer	Activision, Inc.
Retail Price	$39.95

Ratings

Instructions	Not Available
Features	9
Graphics	9
Sound	10
Challenge	7
Play Value	8.60

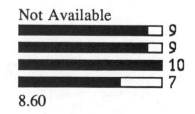

Review

To paraphrase Frank Zappa: "Is there a place for humor in Nintendo games?" If Activision has any say in the matter, the answer is definitely "Yes." The opening for the game is the funniest I've seen.

Swell guys that they are, the Three Stooges have volunteered to raise money to save Ma's Orphanage and keep Ma and her gang from being thrown into the street. If you've watched any of their movies or shorts, you're probably aware just how tough it was for The Stooges to hold a job. They were handymen, but of the worst sort. They'd take any job and, no matter how easy or difficult, mess it up in their own inimitable fashion.

The game is patterned after their onscreen antics. Each job they try is one they worked in the movies. At the start of each turn, an icon bar appears with several jobs, bonuses, and mouse traps. A moving hand flips from job to job. When it's on one you like, press a button to select it. This is easy at the beginning of the game because the selector hand moves slowly. The more days that have passed, the faster the hand moves. If you don't press the button quickly enough, the NES will choose one for you.

The game ends after 30 days have passed or after too many mouse traps have been selected—usually the latter. As near as I can tell, it takes $5,000 or more to win the game.

Instructions

Not available for review.

Features

The jobs portrayed in the game include a cracker-eating contest (the one where the oysters are still alive and eating the crackers before Curly can), waiters (a pie-throwing contest), doctors (making a free-for-all dash down a corridor filled with patients), and Curly's boxing match (where Larry's violin breaks and he must find a radio playing "Three Blind Mice" before Curly is knocked out). The song drives Curly crazy and makes him an unbeatable fighter.

One game choice I really enjoy is "Trivia." You earn $200 for each multiple-choice trivia question you can answer about The Three Stooges, their films, and their personal lives.

Some choices are bonuses. There's nothing you have to do. If you select the "$" symbol, for instance, The Stooges find a sack of money on the street. Pick the safe, and they're rewarded for returning the money they found when a safe cracked open after falling on Curly's head.

There's also a Stooges slapstick fight sequence with Moe slapping and kicking the other two as they duck and squirm. (Other than realism, I'm not sure what effect this has on the game. It doesn't contribute to the score.)

Sound and Graphics

Within the limits of the memory available on an NES cartridge, The Three Stooges game makes use of high-quality digitized sound. There are several spots where The Stooges speak, and their voices are very clear.

The graphics are also good. A few scenes make use of full-screen pictures of The Stooges. They look like the originals and are nicely done. The animated Stooges—the miniature-sized ones—aren't as sharp, but suffice.

Challenge

Some of the scenarios are easily handled. Others, like Larry's boxing match run over and around ladders, boxes, lamp posts, fire hydrants, and sleeping bums, and will take practice to complete. Of course, the more you practice, the more likely you will obtain a respectable score. The mouse trap, however, adds a nasty element of chance to the game. No matter how well you perform the jobs, if you hit too many mouse traps, you'll lose.

Play Value

The Three Stooges is a lot of fun and a great game to show your friends. And the opening sequence will make most adults chuckle, even if they aren't Stooges fans.

Tips, Tricks, and Strategies

- Go for the big money jobs. The easiest, with practice, is the boxing match. Another good one is the Trivia contest.
- Warp speed at the doctors job is fun, but will cost you bucks. The faster you go, the harder it is to avoid the patients.
- Watch Larry's speed in the boxing match run. Too fast and you'll never avoid the obstacles.
- The obstacles in the boxing match run never change. Memorize their order and you'll save precious minutes. And every minute you cut off your time will net you an extra $100.

Tiger-Heli

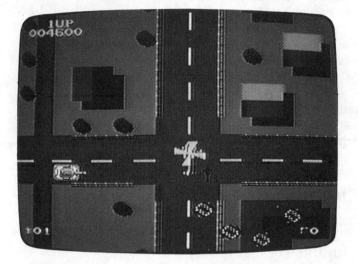

Classification	Arcade
Players	1 or 2
Controller	Standard
Pause	Yes
Restart at Last Level	Yes (see text)
Manufacturer	Acclaim Entertainment
Retail Price	$39.95

Ratings

Instructions	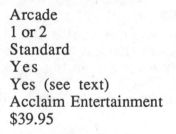	9
Features		10
Graphics		9
Sound		10
Challenge		6
Play Value	8.65	

169

Review

Tiger-Heli is a straight arcade game. No puzzles to solve or secrets to uncover. If you're an ace pilot and can successfully shoot or evade every enemy vehicle you see, you'll be a winner.

Tiger-Heli is a sleuth helicopter, able to instantly reverse direction, and to go undetected by radar. At the start of each mission, it carries unlimited rockets (which it fires four at a time) and two bombs. If you keep your eyes open, you can find and shoot special targets. Some give you extra bombs. Others award a miniature helicopter that links up with Tiger-Heli and increases its fire-power. Additional helicopters are given at 20,000 and multiples of 80,000 points. You can also get a new one by shooting ten bonus blocks.

The object of the game is simple: Stay alive while destroying as many enemy vehicles as possible, and obtain a high score. The game ends when you lose your Tiger-Helis (you start with three of them).

Instructions

The instruction manual is one of the clearest I've seen for an NES game. Each game icon is illustrated—for once, the same way it appears in the game. The manual's only shortcoming is that it doesn't mention the Continue option (see "Tips, Tricks, and Strategies," below).

Features

Try as I might, I couldn't come up with any additional features that would have increased the play value of Tiger-Heli. More weapons might have been added, but keeping it simple—one type for each button—makes sense for the game. It lets you concentrate on the arcade action without having to learn and remember odd button/control pad combinations.

Sound and Graphics

In some scenes, Tiger-Heli uses solid background colors, which, if you've examined other games, are beautiful on the NES even if they are devoid of detail. Other scenes, particularly those in the military airports, provide a tremendous amount of detail. Only the scenes with grass and dirt are a little below par.

The designers did an equally good job on sound effects, although they're limited to gunfire and explosions.

Challenge

Without using the Continue trick described below, it's pretty hard to get to any of the really advanced scenes. And without rapid fire, you'll find it difficult to get past the All-Terrain Attack Modules, particularly when they start ganging up on you in pairs. With the Continue option, however, you'll find the going much easier, even though playing for score quickly loses its point.

Play Value

Tiger-Heli represents the shooting type of arcade game at its best. There's plenty of action, lots of things to shoot, and a requirement of some strategy to keep from being quickly destroyed. Once they get the hang of it, even younger kids can get some play out of it. If you're into mass destruction without the bloodshed that frequently accompanies this type of game, you'll like Tiger-Heli.

Tips, Tricks, and Strategies

- The most frustrating part of Tiger-Heli is having to start over at the beginning of each new game. But you don't have to! To restart from the last screen, press and hold down the A, B, and Start buttons as soon as the game ends.
- Don't worry about beating Tiger-Heli. You can't; there's no end to the game. The object is only to get as many points as you can before being destroyed.
- Learn where enemy objects appear. Every time you start over, they'll be in exactly the same places.
- Mastery of Tiger-Heli depends largely on your ability to dodge and fire. The easiest way, of course, is to shoot the enemy before it can get off its first shot. If you can't do this, let it shoot first, dodge out of the way, and quickly line up your shot and fire.

■ Each time an enemy fires, it always pauses before attempting to lock onto you again. Shoot it during the pause.

■ If you get too close to an enemy without firing, Tiger-Heli will often unleash its bombs to protect you. Don't waste them this way! Try to save bombs for groups of boats or tanks, and the all-terrain attack modules.

Zelda II: The Adventure of Link

Classification	Adventure
Players	1
Controller	Standard
Pause	Yes
Restart at Last Level	Yes, via battery backup
Manufacturer	Nintendo of America, Inc.
Retail Price	$39.95

Ratings

Instructions		10
Features		10
Graphics		8
Sound		9
Challenge		10
Play Value	9.55	

Review

Princess Zelda lies asleep in her palace, the result of a terrible spell. Her brave guardian Link must journey through the land of Hyrule and restore six special Crystals to their rightful place in six stone statues that are in heavily guarded palaces. Only by doing so and surviving the challenge of the seventh palace can Zelda be awakened.

Zelda II is an adventure. Special objects are hidden everywhere, and clues must be unravelled to succeed. Link's power grows as his character develops. By defeating enemies and finding power-up objects, his experience points increase. Once he has accumulated a sufficient number, they can be traded for additional life, magic, or attacking strength.

Instructions

Unlike the instructions for the original Zelda (which gave away so many secrets that it was tough keeping them all straight), Zelda II's instructions tell you only how to play the game and little else. The process of discovery is up to you and your wits.

Features

There are two areas of emphasis in Zelda II. First, as in the original, there are hundreds of creatures to battle. Second, there are towns and secret spots where Link will encounter villagers who will offer him clues, give him special powers and fighting abilities, and restore his life and magic. If you don't explore carefully, you may miss an important clue or never find a critical object.

There are powers galore in the game. The ability to cast magic spells (jumping, shield, fairy, and so on) is bestowed on you by kindly wizards—if you can find them. Special objects (candle, hammer, and the magic glove) play a prominent role, too.

Like the original, Zelda II includes a battery within the cartridge that stores the state of up to three games. After choosing the Save option in the main menu, if you hold in the NES' Reset button while turning the unit off, the current game will be saved. Within the game, if Link loses all his lives, you can Continue as often you wish. Powers and weapons are retained, but Link must begin his travels from the game's starting point rather than from where he was recently defeated.

Sound and Graphics

I enjoyed the music in Zelda II. It has an urgent quality about it that fits well with the game. The sound effects are pretty standard, with the exception of the "fwing" that Link's sword makes when it's thrown.

The graphics have come a long way since the release of the original Legends of Zelda. Instead of a looking like Munchkins, Link and his adversaries are much more realistic. There's still room for improvement, though. The characters are decidedly fuzzy.

Challenge

Zelda II is an extremely challenging game. First, you must decipher clues and, after searching carefully, find the special objects and earn the abilities that are necessary to continue in the game. Since Hyrule is a large country with many secret areas, searching blindly will take weeks. To get anywhere, clues must be found and followed. Second, successful combat requires knowing your enemies and their weaknesses. Discovering this must be done the hard way—by slugging it out, trying various attacks, and using different spells. And if Link loses his final life while combating the guardian of a palace, he'll have to make his way back to the that palace and defeat the same enemies again just to continue.

Play Value

Zelda II: The Adventure of Link offers outstanding play value. It's an excellent adventure that will give most gamers weeks of fine play. Without tips, however, progress will usually be slow. (Note: *Players must be able to read. Young children will enjoy playing Zelda II, but won't get far without help reading the onscreen clues.*)

Tips, Tricks, and Strategies

■ As in the original Zelda, if your life force is at full strength, you can attack many enemies from a safe distance by throwing your sword. Use this tactic as often as possible.

■ To build points the easy way, let a small enemy catch you on the plain outside the castle where Zelda sleeps. The only attackers that will appear will be five Bits; two on one side of the screen and three on the other. You can move back and forth from one end of the screen to the other, and new Bits will appear. As you defeat them, you will slowly gather enough points to advance your life, magic, or attacking power.

■ The Stalfos are weak-kneed adversaries.

■ The candle is in the first palace.

■ To beat the Ironknuckles, don't just slug it out toe to toe. Jump up and hit them in the head a few times. (Note that you'll connect more often by pressing forward and swinging.)

■ Use the jumping and shield spells to give you enough of an advantage to defeat the guardian of the first palace.

■ Explore every inch of forest, desert, and swamp. Special objects are hidden there. There's a 1-UP in the desert next to the graveyard, for instance. In particular, you should make a point of entering any square that is different from the surrounding terrain. [GJ]

■ Visit the towns again after conquering a palace or finding magic objects. Sometimes the town folk haven't said all they have to say.

■ Explore all the caves. Some are tunnels, some have experience, and some contain items necessary in other parts of the game. [GJ]

■ Contrary to the clue provided in the game, you won't find the magic hammer in a swamp. It's in a cave.

■ Don't forget that the hammer can also be used for clearing out sections of the forest. One area hides a town.

■ Try hitting the statues in front and inside of the palaces for a quick magic boost. Note: You won't always be rewarded. Sometimes they come to life and want to fight! [KB]

- The flute makes the spider disappear. *[GJ]*
- Strange things can happen when you cast a spell. Try it when you reach a dead end in a particular town. *[GJ]*
- Fire will damage any monster that the sword cannot. *[GJ]*
- Boots let you walk on water. *[GJ]*
- The water is a maze with invisible walls. *[GJ]*
- In one town, you can go down a chimney to reach a weapons master. *[GJ]*
- You must go through a maze to reach one palace. One of the maze paths will take you there with only a single encounter. *[GJ]*
- If you don't have a key, you can go through keyholes with the fairy spell. *[GJ]*

If you've given up on *Zelda II: The Adventures of* Link, see *"Super Secrets"* for more tips.

PART II
Short Takes

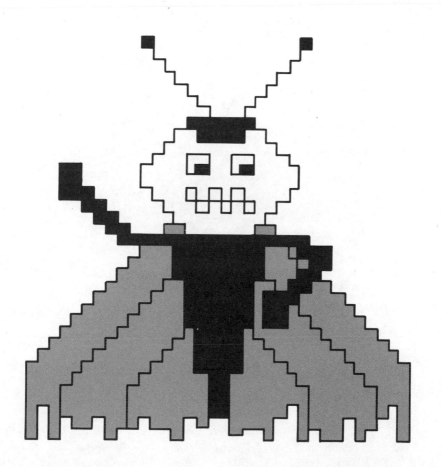

Short Takes

Because of the lateness of their arrival or their complexity, it wasn't possible to fully play-test and review some games. Rather than exclude them, many appear in this section of the book. Although the reviews are short, you should be able to get a good idea of whether the games are worth further consideration. Even with the limited play time spent on these games, I was frequently able to come up with a useful tip or two (or five).

Please keep in mind that some of these games were prototypes and were examined without the benefit of a manual. Forgive me if it turns out that the tips I discovered are occasionally included within the games' published instructions and that the characters' names aren't always given.

Athena

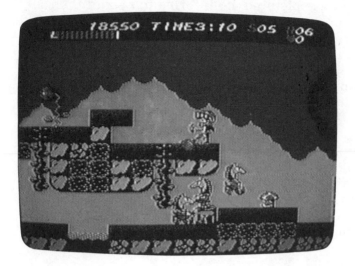

Classification   Arcade
Manufacturer   SNK Corp. of America
Price $34.95

Impression

Finally there's a game with a girl as the heroine! Actually,
although she looks like a little girl, Athena is really the
Goddess of Wisdom. (I guess she's just small for her age.)
Bored with her life in the castle, she has entered the Fanta-
sy World outside in search of adventure.

   If there were a prize for the strangest-looking charac-
ters in a video game, Athena would surely be nominated.
Some of the nastier ones are Kat, odd little men who shoot
arrows at Athena, and Gabby, horse men with swords.
There's also Joss, a sort of fuzzy pickle that wields a mace.
Interesting, to say the least.

The manual provides the basic information about Athena, but leaves much for the player to discover. Many weapons and special objects are not shown. Although some of the enemies are pictured, no information about their attacking style or strength is provided.

Although Athena has every appearance of being a children's game, it will probably prove to be too tough for most young kids. (It took me six hours to make it through the first three worlds!) Unlimited Continues help a little, but only if you make it out of the first world.

Tips, Tricks, and Strategies

- Watch Athena's Strength and Hit Points as you pick up new weapons and other objects. You'll quickly learn which ones are the most powerful.
- If you pick up the iron ball and chain, try to hold onto it. It's great for smashing rocks.
- Avoid the object that looks like a glove. It's a very weak weapon.
- Picking up the blue hourglass restores your time; the red one makes you lose time.
- Keep an eye peeled for the magic lamp. If you can find the proper exit, you can get to the next level without confronting the super monster at the end of the current world.
- Find the magic scroll. It gives you a disc-like weapon (I call it the Frisbee of Death) that can easily take out enemies or an entire row of rocks with each toss.

Jackal

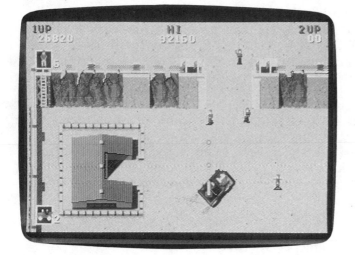

Classification   Arcade
Manufacturer   Konami Industry Co. Ltd.
Price $39.95

The Jackals are an elite jeep squad composed of Green Berets. They and their all-terrain attack jeeps have been sent back to Vietnam by the President. Their mission is to rescue the P.O.W.s that still remain.

Rescuing prisoners is a three-step process: Blow up the buildings they are being held in, load them into your jeep, and transport them safely to a helicopter landing pad where they'll be whisked away to freedom. There's a landing pad in each scenario. If your vehicle is destroyed on the way, the prisoners have a tendency to wander off. Collect them quickly and be on your way again.

The enemy will try every trick in the book to stop you, throwing tanks, planes, helicopters, cannons, submarines, and lasers in your path. You're hardly defenseless, though.

Your quick reflexes, paired with your machine gun and hand grenades should be sufficient for you to get by. If they aren't, you can earn a bazooka by performing the correct action.

Jackal can be played by one or two players simultaneously. In simultaneous play, each controls his own assault jeep. Play takes place in six enemy territories, labelled Checkpoint Alpha through Checkpoint Zulu.

Impression

Jackal has a lot of entertainment value. Advancement is mainly a matter of getting used to controlling the jeep and learning to fire instinctively—and doing it right. Two-player games are also fun. Although you can still compete for score, helping each other make it through the checkpoints is more enjoyable.

Tips, Tricks, and Strategies

■ If you can't shoot the enemy soldiers, run them over. It works just as well.
■ Bombs can be tossed over walls. *[GJ]*
■ Shoot everywhere. Sometimes you'll uncover a secret emblem that, when destroyed, demolishes all the enemies on screen. *[ES]*
■ Shoot the columns and statues in Checkpoint Baker. Some will give you a surprise.
■ The lasers in Checkpoint Charlie cannot be destroyed. See how fast you can run. *[GJ]*
■ It takes two bombs to destroy each of the guns on the ship in Checkpoint Charlie. *[GJ]*
■ Water in Checkpoint Delta slows you down. *[GJ]*
■ Shoot the engine in Checkpoint Delta to demolish the entire train. *[GJ]*
■ Only direct hits have any effect on the giant helicopter in Checkpoint Delta. *[GJ]*
■ Watch out for land mines in Checkpoint Tango.
■ In Checkpoint Tango, you can blow up the doors only when they're open. This disables the electric gate. *[GJ]*

If you've given up on *Jackal*, see "Super Secrets" for more tips.

Kid Kool

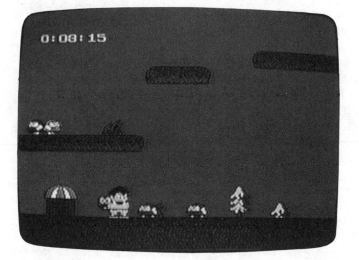

Classification	Arcade
Manufacturer	Vic Tokai, Inc.
Price	$41.95

Kid Kool has much in common with Super Mario Bros. Because it's so similar, comparisons are inevitable (and unavoidable). Like Super Mario Bros., Kid Kool is divided into Worlds and Levels (1-1, 1-2, and so on), and has hidden objects that must be found.

Instead of fireballs, Kid Kool has Wickie, a fuzzy little ball of fur with a permanently silly expression that the Kid carries under his arm. When enemies appear, the Kid just tosses Wickie at them to bowl them over. Then Wickie magically (and automatically) hops back into the Kid's arms. Like fireballs, Wickie can be lost. The first time Kid Kool is touched by an enemy, Wickie disappears. If it happens a second time, the Kid loses one of his lives and the level must be started over.

Rather than display a score, the game is based on time. The Kid has three days to complete a mission for the king. As major time intervals are reached, the background screen color changes. If you can find them, hidden Time Downs reduce the time on the clock. Watch out, though. There are also Time Ups that increase it.

Kid Kool leaves little room for error. Jumps, in many cases, must be to exact squares or the Kid will fall into the water. At the very least, a single misplaced jump will often force you to take a different and usually more difficult route. To the player's benefit, there are unlimited Continues and each starts at the specific level where the Kid died, rather than at the beginning of the World.

Impression

Unless the manual reveals some significant tricks that I wasn't able to uncover (and, hopefully, this will be the case), you'll find that progress in Kid Kool is slow. After playing the game for two weeks, we were only able to get to level 1-3. It is fun, though, and the characters are cute.

Tips, Tricks, and Strategies

■ Watch the placement of beach houses just before a stretch of water. They usually indicate the spot Kid Kool must start running from in order to jump across the water.
■ When crossing a large body of water, Kid Kool can run on the surface. Wait until he makes two or three skips and then hit the jump button.
■ Slide through patches of grass to see if something is hidden there. You'll usually find a Wickie this way near the beginning of each level.

Operation Wolf

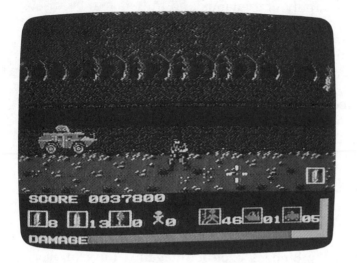

Classification	Arcade
Manufacturer	Taito Software
Price	$44.99

In this game, you're in command of a team of U.S. soldiers that have been sent to South America to free hostages taken captive by terrorists. Using your controller alone or in combination with the NES Zapper light gun, you must destroy the terrorists and their vehicles while leaving the hostages unharmed. Operation Wolf has four levels, each with six missions to be completed by defeating all the terrorists present.

If you're playing with the Zapper, press its trigger to fire bullets and press the trigger and B button together to launch grenades. Because it's hard to hit the enemies with the Zapper, though, you may want to try this one with the controller alone. In controller-only play, crosshairs appear onscreen and are directed with the control pad.

As you play, a lifeline at the bottom of the screen shows your hit status. When it becomes completely red, the game ends. Life can be restored by finding power drinks. Similarly, your supply of grenades and bullets can be increased by shooting special objects that appear. Although it's hard to keep an eye on them at the same time you shoot, other indicators onscreen show weapons status, prisoners rescued, and the number of enemy soldiers and vehicles remaining in the mission.

If you succeed in completing the missions, you'll receive a speech from the President assessing your team's performance (which depends on the number of prisoners you rescued).

Impression

The graphics in Operation Wolf are weak, particularly when displaying special items like grenades, power-ups, and so on. Once you recognize the general shape of each (pause the game and check each icon against the manual), the game gets easier.

Play with the Zapper is extremely difficult, even in the first mission. The enemy soldiers are small and tough to hit, particularly given the fast pace of the game. On the other hand, if you enjoy the rifle and pistol-shooting games found in arcades, you'll probably like Operation Wolf. It has the same flavor.

Tips, Tricks, and Strategies

- When a soldier lobs a bomb at you, shoot it before it explodes. You'll damage the soldiers rather than getting hit yourself.
- In the jungle scene, don't shoot the dynamite until soldiers are near it.
- If you're having trouble getting anywhere at all, try running Operation Wolf entirely in slow motion. This is one of the few games where a controller with slow motion actually helps.

Stealth ATF

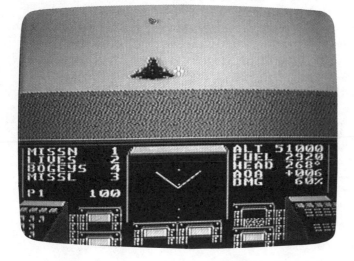

Classification Arcade
Manufacturer Activision
Price $39.95

Picture yourself in the pilot's seat of a Stealth bomber.
Your code name is "Shadow," and you've just received orders to pilot your craft to a mission in the Middle East.
With the Stealth's rapid-fire machine gun and eight heat-seeking missiles, you must take out four enemy fighter
planes to complete your first mission. Good luck, Shadow.
It will either be dogfight or dogmeat before the day is over.

The Stealth is flown from the pilot's perspective. All
you can see is your instrument panel and whatever sights
your forward view panel offers. Luckily, the plane is
equipped with a sophisticated control panel, indicating
your altitude and angle to the ground, and the positions of
any bogeys in the area (via radar). To help hide you from

the enemy planes (and switch off that annoying music), the plane has a silent or stealth mode. All you can hear is the quiet drone of the ship's engine.

It's easy to get the hang of shooting down the enemies. If you manage to hit them all without taking any damage, several more show up for a fast bonus round. Then comes the hard part: landing the plane. Get it right and you'll move on to more difficult missions—with night flying and more bogeys. Get it wrong and your plane will burst into flames. Stealths cost the U.S. government big bucks. Destroy three of them and you're out of the game. (They don't suggest taking it out of your pay for the next 10,000 years or so, but they do state that driving a bus might be more your speed.)

Stealth ATF can be played by one or two players, each playing on separate turns. The graphics on takeoff and landing are superb. Once in the sky, there's not much of interest in either the air or on the ground (which is shown as an unchanging dirty brown pattern).

Impression

I wish there had been a manual available when I played Stealth ATF, but I don't think it would have helped. What I really need is practice on my landings. Stealth ATF isn't a fantastic game, but if you like the idea of being able to chase down enemy planes while proving your prowess in the pilot's seat, you'll have fun with it.

Tips, Tricks, and Strategies

- At the beginning of each mission, the bogeys come straight at you. Your best move is change course a bit, so you don't start out with immediate damage.
- You don't have to wait for the fighter planes to come to you. Any time you pass them, you can quickly get back at them by flipping the plane over 180 degrees.
- When the "locked on" indicator flashes and you fire, try to keep the enemy plane on screen. If you can, your heat-seeking missile will take it out. Let it slip out of sight and the missile will slide harmlessly past.
- Stealth ATF is a great game for using the Zoomer controller.

PART III
Extra Help

Super Secrets

The information in this section will do a lot more than help you improve your scores. It will give you a real head start at beating a game. It's here, for instance, where you'll learn high-level passwords that will let you jump ahead in a game, tricks to gain additional lives, or the location of critical objects.

Some may feel that this spoils the game or is the same as cheating. What it's intended to do is give those players who are stuck or have given up a way to bring some life back into a game. These aren't just hints. They're last resorts and should be treated that way!

So you don't read what's printed here by mistake, all secrets are printed in "mirror" type. Unless you have very good eyes, you'll only be able to read these tips by holding the pages up to a mirror.

Last Warning: Don't use this information if you don't have to!

1943: The Battle of Midway

■ The music changes when your energy drops below 20. Use this as a signal to power up. [JS]
■ Pick up two boomerangs in a row for a super-powered weapon. [ES]
■ Want to try a higher level? Here are passwords for levels 5, 6, 7, and 8: S8JGN, ZFJGX, IFPGD, PEPG8.

Adventures of Lolo

■ To finish level 6-2, you need to use an Emerald Framer to block two squares at once.
■ To complete level 6-3, you must lure the Leeper into the correct spot and then make him fall asleep.
■ You can beat level 9-1 with sufficient speed, but there's an easier way. If you wait in just the right spot in the square track at the bottom, the Alma will race past you and go up the right side towards the treasure chest. You'll have plenty of time to reach the heart framer. [JS]
■ Use these passwords to start at the beginning of level 5, 6, 7, 8, or 9: CJZM, CPZH, CYYZ, DGYQ, DMYJ.

195

Athena

■ In the World of Forest, stand on the first small mushroom that you can and push down on the control pad. You will receive a giant flame sword. [G]

Bionic Commando

■ Continues must be earned. When moving from one area to the next, your helicopter will occasionally meet an enemy truck. In the fight that follows, some characters you defeat will leave an eagle behind. You will be awarded one Continue for each eagle you pick up. [JuS]

Blaster Master

■ If you can't defeat the bullet-shooting idol in Area 1, it's because you have to destroy the boss for the area first. The idol is the entrance to Area 2. [ES]

Bubble Bobble

■ The password for level 99 is CE]]. Completing this level is critical to finishing the first half of the game.
■ To beat level 99 and continue the game, you must grab the crystal ball and go through the secret exit. (It's a door behind the Hullaballoon.) [JS]

Castlevania II: Simon's Quest

■ To get to a new mansion, hold the heart when you get on the ferry. [G]
■ Kneel at the very edge of the lake while holding the crystal and wait ten seconds. [G]
■ Kneel at the edge of the Jam Wastelands while holding the crystal and wait ten seconds. [G]

City Connection

■ To keep a balloon from scrolling off the screen and give you time to catch it, move your car in the same direction. Reverse direction if the balloon starts to scroll off in the opposite direction.

Clash at Demonhead

■ Use the Powerball to defeat Rowdy.
■ Dive into the well on Route 15 to get to the desert fortress.
■ You can exchange gold for cash on Route 22.
■ You'll find the demon inside the mountain on Route 39.
■ If you want to start near the end, try this super password: CTULA 741MF 81Q9S DW1QP 2V216 48645. All that's left is to build up force and fight the final battle above Route 42.

Double Dragon

■ To beat the two Abobos that pop out of the wall in Mission 3, just use flying jump kicks. [G]

Golgo 13

■ Enemy agents in the street scenes wear sunglasses. [ES]
■ In the helicopter sniper sequence, the target is in the building to your left—not the one you first see.

Jackal

■ Rescue blinking hostages for power-ups. They always come out of buildings in a downward direction, instead of from the sides. [G]

Karnov

■ Use the boomerang to quickly dispatch the Leaping Lizard at the end of Stage 1. [ES]
■ The shield is good protection from the dinosaur in Stage 3. [ES]

■ It takes two well-placed bombs to destroy the Snake Woman. [ES]
■ You can defeat the dinosaur in Stage 5 by climbing the ladder and shooting it in the head. [ES]

The Legend of Zelda

■ The sword is hidden under a gravestone in the cemetery. [G]
■ You need the whistle to defeat Digdogger. [G]
■ When it opens, shoot arrows at Gohma's eye. [G]
■ The whistle will reveal dungeon level 7 to you. [G]
■ The entrance to the Level 9 labyrinth is on Spectacle Rock on Death Mountain. Set off a bomb on the left rock to reveal it. [AS]
■ There is a second built-in adventure. To start it, enter the name ZELDA as a new player.

Legendary Wings

■ You must destroy the final two Shoguns at the end of the first part of each stage to make the dragon appear. It takes three hits to do this. [G]
■ You must kill the demon in the final stage and then pass through it. [G]

Mappy-Land

■ To complete stage 1–8, Mappy must find six pieces of cheese, not five. One is hidden in a picture.
■ You can press down on the control pad to reduce the height of Mappy's bounces on the trampolines.

Mega Man II

■ If you're having trouble getting started, try Bubble Man or Air Man. Either can be beaten without special powers.
■ If you want to destroy the Lantern Fish, shoot its antenna. [ES]

198

- Use tornado power to take care of Wood Man.
- Save up your energy crystals for Metal Man.
- Heat Man doesn't care for bubbles.
- You can use the Flying Fish eggs and Crazy Cannons to your advantage in the final area. If you're short on some powers, do this. Use your standard weapon (P) to shoot, and then switch to the other power before picking up the energy pellets.
- First you race the dragon. Then you fight him.
- Guts-Dozer can be beaten by standing on the front of his vehicle, then jumping up and shooting him in the head. It takes a lot of shots.
- If you'd like a few super powers to start off with, use this password: A1, C4, D1, D3, D5, E1, E2, E3, E4. If you want to go directly to Dr. Wiley's level, enter: A1, B2, B4, C1, C5, D1, D3, E3, E5.

Metal Gear

- When pitted against Twin Shot, move Solid Snake to the upper right-hand corner. Once there, he can't be hit. [G]
- To get the rocket launcher, you must call several times. [G]
- When fighting the big boss in Outer Heaven, stand still next to the upper left-hand crate. The boss will merely move up and down on the right as you shoot at him. You must still dodge his bullets, however. [G]
- It's hard to get anywhere without decent weapons. Here's a password that will give you a head start: 4ZZ2H K2R)D M3]]C B11S6 NH5TK. [G]

Mickey Mousecapade

- You can go straight from Spring to Fall in the Woods. After you pass the second tree with a door, you'll come to a pit. Shoot near the bottom of this tree to open a secret doorway. (It's just before the Start line.) [ES]
- To defeat the pirate captain, make Minnie climb the ladder by herself, leaving Mickey down below. Then start throwing stars. Minnie cannot be hit. [G]

199

RoboWarrior

■ Don't bother using the beam gun on the evil lords. It would take 1500 hits just to destroy Globula. The most effective weapons—in order—are megaton bombs, hyper missiles, and bombs.
■ To complete level 3-1, go straight up the middle.
■ In level 6-1, the key is hidden in the water.

Super Mario Bros.

■ To get to the Warp Zone that leads to level 8, go to World 4-2. Jump up in the right place and you'll reveal two invisible blocks. Jump onto them and punch the leftmost block over Mario's head. A beanstalk will appear that will take you to the Warp Zone.
■ At the end of World 3-1, you will find two turtles coming down the stairs. If you jump on the second one while it's on the steps, it will turn into a shell. Continue jumping on it for more lives. (Very difficult to master.) [DB, IP]

Super Mario Bros. 2

■ How about two power blocks instead of one? In World 1-1, pick up the first potion you find and drop it next to the power block below. Grab the power block while you're in sub-space and you'll still have it when you return. [ES]
■ To defeat Ostro, jump on his eggs as they come at you and throw them back at him.
■ Pidgit looks like a flying manta ray. Since he's really just a bird on a flying carpet, you can jump on his head and toss him away. The carpet will be yours for a free ride.
■ To warp straight from World 1-3 to 4-1, drop a potion by the jar at the end of the scene and climb in from Sub-space.
■ Mouser can be beaten by catching the bombs he tosses, jumping up, and dropping them on the ledge behind him.
■ To get past the spikes in World 4-2, find something to carry you.
■ You can warp to World 6-1 if you drop the potion by a jar about halfway through World 4-2 and climb in from Sub-space. [GI]
■ The key to the door in World 6-1 is in the fifth jar from the end. [GI]

200

- To get many extra lives on the slot machine, press the button as soon as the reels start moving. More often than not the first reel will be a cherry. [G]

Teenage Mutant Ninja Turtles

- Boomerangs can be shared. When one of the turtles gets them, have him toss several at once. Before they return, switch characters and let the new turtle catch them. [ES]

Zelda II: The Adventure of Link

- The magic glove can be found in the second palace.
- To reach the island palace, Link must fall through a hole in the cemetery.
- There are hidden pits in the Great Palace. Sometimes it's good to go down them. One is hidden under some rocks that you must break. [G]
- When fighting your shadow at the end of the game, move all the way to the left. You can hit the shadow through its shield. [BM], [G]

Game Play Value Ratings

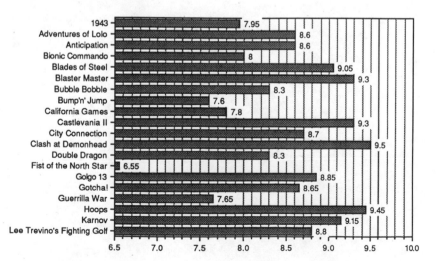

1943	7.95
Adventures of Lolo	8.6
Anticipation	8.6
Bionic Commando	8
Blades of Steel	9.05
Blaster Master	9.3
Bubble Bobble	8.3
Bump'n' Jump	7.6
California Games	7.8
Castlevania II	9.3
City Connection	8.7
Clash at Demonhead	9.5
Double Dragon	8.3
Fist of the North Star	6.55
Golgo 13	8.85
Gotcha!	8.65
Guerrilla War	7.65
Hoops	9.45
Karnov	9.15
Lee Trevino's Fighting Golf	8.8

Game Play Value Ratings

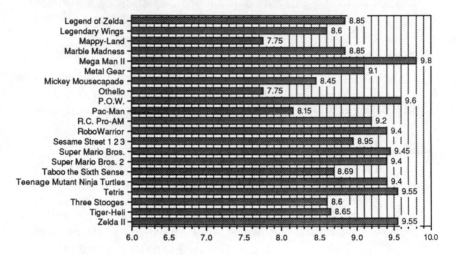

Legend of Zelda	8.85
Legendary Wings	8.6
Mappy-Land	7.75
Marble Madness	8.85
Mega Man II	9.8
Metal Gear	9.1
Mickey Mousecapade	8.45
Othello	7.75
P.O.W.	9.6
Pac-Man	8.15
R.C. Pro-AM	9.2
RoboWarrior	9.4
Sesame Street 1 2 3	8.95
Super Mario Bros.	9.45
Super Mario Bros. 2	9.4
Taboo the Sixth Sense	8.69
Teenage Mutant Ninja Turtles	9.4
Tetris	9.55
Three Stooges	8.6
Tiger-Heli	8.65
Zelda II	9.55

PART IV
Controllers

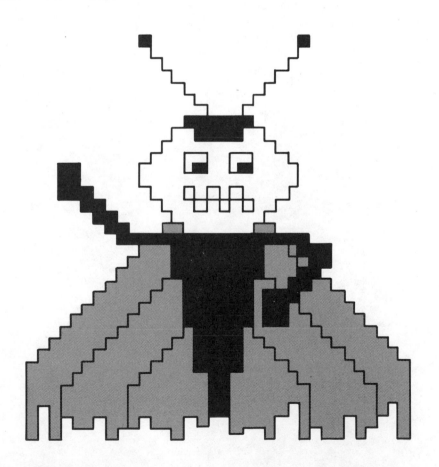

About the Controller Reviews

This section of the book includes reviews and descriptions of some popular replacement controllers for the NES. Many add new features that can be used to improve scores, such as remote control operation, rapid-fire, and slow motion.

Like the game cartridges, each controller is rated on several useful criteria, so you can quickly judge whether it's the one for you. Rating categories include *Construction* (how well it's designed and made), *Features* (included options), *Responsiveness* (how accurately it responds to your touch), and *Play Value* (a summary score based on equal weightings of the other three ratings). As with games, each controller rating uses a ten-point scale, where 0 is poor and 10 is excellent.

Each controller's Features rating started with a base score of 5 for a controller with the same features as the standard NES controller. A point was added to the score for possessing each of the following special features: rapid-fire, 360-degree control, slow motion, remote control, and two-player mode.

To make picking a new controller even easier, there's a Features Comparison Chart that shows the features each controller has and its price. You'll find the chart helpful if you've decided to look only at controllers with specific features or in a particular price range.

Controller Features

The basic Nintendo set comes with a pair of standard game controllers. More advanced sets add a Zapper light gun for shooting games and a Power Pad for exercise-oriented games. Whether your controllers have worn out or you just want to add a competitive edge to your game playing, there is a variety of replacements to choose from. Here are the features that the various controllers offer, in addition to the standard buttons and control pad.

Remote Control

Remote control lets you operate the NES from distances as far away as 30 feet. The controller has two parts. First, an infrared-sensing unit plugs into the controller port of the NES. The controller, the second component, emits infrared light each time a button is pressed or the control pad is moved, and this information is transmitted to the sensing unit. The remote control feature works like the remote controls you use for your TV, VCR, or stereo. Because each controller must be able to send out light, they are all powered by batteries.

The main advantages of remote control are the greater distances over which it can operate and not having to worry about tangled cords. The biggest disadvantage is that, in order to work, nothing must come between the controller and the sensing unit. If your dog strolls across the floor, Mario dies!

Bottom Line: If you want to avoid the clutter of cords, remote control is the way to go. Personally, I find that playing from a distance of 20 feet (even sitting comfortably on a couch) is too far away for interaction with the game. An extra-long cord is often just as good.

360-Degree Control

The control pad on the standard NES controller is adequate for most games. A joystick, trackball, or thumbwheel gives you additional control. You can move easily in any direction—not just left, right, up, or down.

The disadvantages of 360-degree control are that some games only respond correctly to straight vertical or horizontal movements—which can be tough to make with a joystick, trackball, or thumbwheel. There's nothing more frustrating than watching Pac-Man get swallowed by a ghost because you didn't press "up" as carefully as you thought you had.

Some players may find a joystick uncomfortable, particularly for long playing sessions. Most joysticks are considerably larger than the standard controllers, and are easiest to play with when mounted on a table or resting on the floor.

Bottom Line: Recognizing that 360-degree control isn't suitable for every game, it's still an excellent feature for a second controller.

Rapid-Fire

Rapid-fire, speed-up, or "turbo" mode works just as if you were pressing the A or B button as fast as possible. At the simplest level, some controllers provide rapid-fire as an on/off switch. More advanced controllers offer two or three speed choices. The most advanced ones use dials or sliding switches, letting you select any speed you like for the Λ and B buttons individually.

Speed-up is often a big help in shooting games. All you have to do is hold the button down and the controller will automatically lay down fire as fast as it can. It's usable in a large number of games, and is unquestionably one of the most important features available today.

If you're considering this option, you'll find that many games work better with separate A and B speed-up controls. Some just won't work if both buttons are on rapid-fire.

Bottom Line: For most games, this is the feature to have.

Slow Motion

Slow motion works by rapidly pausing and restarting the game. For some games, this will give you just enough time to shoot that last monster or avoid falling into the pit. For others, it can't be used at all because the game locks or the screen flicker is unbearable.

Bottom Line: Although a good idea, slow motion is a seldom-used feature. Although the monsters may be slowed up, so are you.

Multiple Buttons

To accommodate both left- and right-handed players, some controllers have two sets of A and B buttons, one set on each side. Obviously, if you don't have left-handed friends or brothers and sisters, this feature won't be much use to you.

Bottom Line: If you're not left-handed or ambidextrous, you can pass on this feature.

☐ About the Controller Reviews

Suction Cups

Some controllers, because of their sizes, shapes, or designs, are best used in a fixed position. This is particularly important for remote control units, since they must be kept in careful alignment with the sensing unit. Suction cups allow you to stick the controller to a table and keep it from sliding around while you're trying to concentrate on the game.

　　Bottom Line: This is a good feature for joysticks and remote control units.

Two-Player Control

A few controllers can work for two-player games. Generally, you must flip a switch each time players change, so you have to be quick. *(Note: This type of controller cannot be used by itself for two-player simultaneous games; you'll still need two of them.)*

　　Bottom Line: Since the most advanced controllers cost more, having two-player capability is a nice way to save money. Rather than buying an extra one for your brother (or fighting over who gets to use the expensive one), you can just pass it back and forth when your turn comes.

Chapter Organization

The first section of the chapter rates and reviews general-purpose replacement controllers for the NES. Controllers in this section, while adding many useful and innovative features, are intended to be useful for a wide variety of games.

　　The second section discusses special-purpose controllers. Such controllers are frequently usable for only a subset of NES games. A few general-purpose controllers, because of their revolutionary design or features, have also been placed in this section.

　　A third brief section discusses NES accessories that, while cute and interesting, have nothing whatsoever to do with game play. I just felt like tossing them in.

　　The chapter concludes with a Summary Chart of Play Value Ratings, showing you the overall rating for each controller reviewed.

Standard Controllers

Acclaim Entertainment, Inc.

Name	Wireless Infrared Remote Controller
Price	$39.95

Ratings

Construction		10
Features		7
Responsiveness		9
Play Value	8.67	

Review

With dimensions only slightly larger than the standard NES controller, the Wireless Infrared Remote Controller has the distinction of being one of the smallest remote units. At $39.95 retail, it's tied for least expensive remote controller. Although it uses the same color and type of plastic that the

NES controllers are made of, it appears to be quite sturdy.

The only other feature the Wireless Infrared Remote Controller offers is rapid-fire. Rapid-fire affects both buttons—limiting its utility somewhat—and works with an on/off switch rather than allowing variable settings.

Like other remote units, Acclaim's is battery-powered. It takes 4 AAA batteries. It has a single pair of A and B buttons that are the same size as those on the original NES controller. To preserve battery life, it has a power switch and a small LED that shows when it's on.

One problem with the unit is the length of the cord used to connect the sensor to the NES: It's about 18 inches long. This means two things. First, placement of the sensor is severely restricted. It must either be directly on or next to the NES. If the NES isn't on top of your television (mine isn't), you'll have to aim the controller at something other than the set. Second, because of the cord's short length, it has a tendency to pull the sensor out of alignment with the front of the NES.

If you want a remote control unit and would like to get in as cheaply as possible, the Wireless Infrared Remote Controller is one possibility.

Bandai America, Inc.

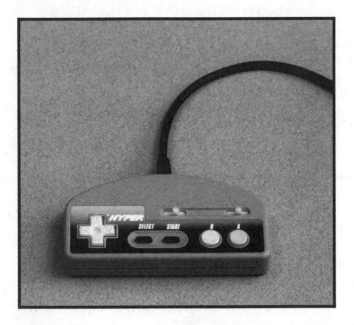

Name	Hyper
Price	$29.99

Ratings

Construction		9
Features		6
Responsiveness		8
Play Value	7.67	

Review

Picture the NES controller with separate A and B button
rapid-fire controls and a rounded front edge, and you have
the Bandai Hyper controller. The rounded front edge has a
purpose. It's grooved and makes a good resting place for
the index finger of each hand; this makes it a bit more
functional than the NES design. On the other hand, there's
nothing new about the design and shape of the control pad,
Select, Start, or A and B buttons.

211

The speed of rapid-fire can be set for each button individually with sliding switches. Either the Hyper's control for rapid-fire is more powerful than that of other controllers or it's poorly calibrated. On some games, you'll find that one or both of the settings can only be pushed to about the half-way mark. Past that point and the button stops working—implying that Hyper may be toggling the button faster than the NES can handle it. Not being able to safely push the slides to the top makes it necessary to reset them for each game. For this reason, Hyper wasn't a favorite of mine.

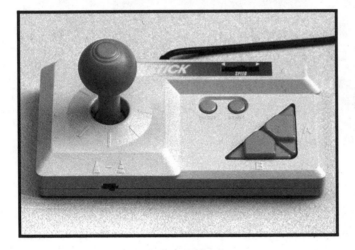

Name	Hyper Stick
Price	$34.99

Ratings

Construction	10
Features	7
Responsiveness	10
Play Value	9.0

Review

The Hyper Stick is a standard joystick for the NES. Its only feature is rapid-fire, which, although the speed is variable, affects both A and B buttons simultaneously. They cannot be adjusted individually.

Hyper Stick really excels in its design. The joystick is made of a soft, easy-to-hold plastic. The A and B buttons are made of the same material, and are oversized, making them simple to hit and easy on your fingers for extended play. It's a very comfortable unit to use.

If comfort is your thing, you'll find that Hyper Stick is a great joystick to fall back on when your fingers are too sore to use any other controller. Or maybe that's a good time to take a break.

Name	Mega Controller
Price	$42.99

Ratings

Construction	9
Features	9
Responsiveness	10
Play Value	9.33

Review

The Mega Controller, although it looks somewhat like the standard NES controller, is a breed apart. It includes several features that make it unique among hand-held controllers. First, it contains an LED screen that shows the status of each of the many options that can be set. In addition to rapid-fire and slow motion, you can lock the A and/or B buttons in the down position. The effect is continuous fire without having to press a button. A *pad lock* mode can also be used to lock the control pad into moving continuously in any direction you select.

Next, for games you've already mastered, the Mega provides two options to give yourself a handicap. You can limit the number of times the A or B button can be pressed (*arsenal mode*), or the amount of time a game can be played (between 2 and 120 minutes). If you're already a top gun on a shooting game, for example, see how far you can get once you've set a 15-minute time limit.

A *memory mode* allows the Mega to learn and play back a single password of up to 16 characters. To use it, simply go to a game's password start option, set the Mega for memory mode, and press the control pad and buttons as you normally would to enter the password. The next time you want to use the password, set the Mega for memory mode again and the password will be played back for you. The batteries (4 AAA) allow the password to be remembered between games—even after you turn the Mega off.

Finally, there are two mini games built into the Mega. The first one simply counts the number of times you can press the A and B buttons in ten seconds. If you manage to do this 130 times or more, you get a chance to play the Top Secret game that's part of the controller.

The only flaw in the Mega's design is the size and shape of its buttons. Because they're small, like those on the original NES controller, they can be painful to use for long periods. As an example, although it's a great feature, there aren't many games where you can leave the button safely locked with rapid-fire on. Instead, you have to hold the button down. Some players, like myself, have a tendency to mash the button down to keep the fire at its peak. Over a period of many hours, this equals pain.

Note: Although the Mega only provides two of the five special features that contribute to the Features rating, its score was raised to 9 because of its many unique features.

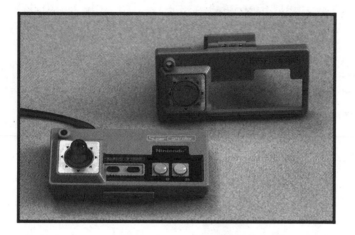

Name	Super Controller
Price	$7.99

Ratings

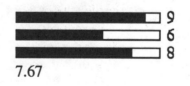

Construction	9
Features	6
Responsiveness	8
Play Value	7.67

Review

The Super Controller isn't a controller at all. It's a case that, when fitted around and over your original NES controllers, gives them a joystick function.

The design is ingenious. The Super Controller is a pair of hinged gray plastic cases that snap snugly over each of your original NES controllers. The Select, Start, A, and B buttons are fully exposed. The control pad is covered by a circular rotating disc that accepts one of two stubby joystick knobs. One is shaped liked a toggle switch and the other is mushroom-shaped. Once fitted with a joystick knob, the NES controller can approximate a joystick function, giving you 360-degree control over screen movements.

In case you want to play without the joystick knob (it may be more comfortable to use just the circular disc with some games), the controller case has an extra hole to hold the knob so it doesn't get lost.

If you're on a budget and want to add a joystick function to your controllers, buying a Super Controller is an inexpensive way to do it.

Beeshu, Inc.

Name	Jazz Stick
Price	$22.99

Ratings

Construction	▇▇▇▇▇▇▇▇▭	9
Features	▇▇▇▇▇▇▭▭	7
Responsiveness	▇▇▇▇▇▇▇▇▭	9
Play Value	8.33	

Review

If your last controller was the standard one that comes with the NES, it will take a some time to get used to the Jazz Stick. All button positions are reversed. The A and B buttons are on the left side with A furthest to the left. Start and Select are at the top with Start on the left. The full-control joystick is set into the right side of the unit. As a right-handed player, I had little trouble adjusting to it, but I occasionally got A and B mixed up. I also found it difficult to quickly press Select or Start at critical points in some games.

There is a solid look and feel to the Jazz Stick. The oversized A and B buttons are easy to hit and comfortable for long playing sessions. There are separate single-position rapid-fire controls for both buttons. An LED lights up to show when each one is in use. This adds nothing to the functionality of the unit, but is a nice touch.

Four suction cups are mounted on the unit's base. Because the Jazz Stick is fairly heavy, you'll find that many games can be played without using them.

The unit's only significant weakness is its cord. With a length of only four feet, plan on playing with your face in the TV set. Of course, if this is already your usual style of play, this won't be a problem. Like many of the controllers manufactured by Beeshu, the Jazz Stick offers several useful features (joystick and rapid-fire) for a moderate price.

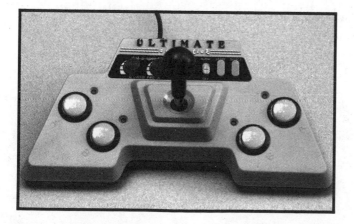

Name	Ultimate Superstick
Price	$39.99

Ratings

Construction		9
Features		8
Responsiveness		10
Play Value	9.00	

Review

The Ultimate Superstick is appropriately named. It contains many popular features that players look for in an NES-compatible joystick. It has separate A and B button rapid-fire control, slow motion, and two sets of A and B buttons for right- or left-handed play. It's a large controller, but five suction cups are permanently mounted on its base to give it stability when it's needed.

The sets of A and B buttons are oversized, making them easy to hit and easy on your fingers. Having the joystick center-mounted makes it equally usable whether you are left- or right-handed. The rapid-fire controls are set by turning dials to let you fine-tune the amount of fire-power needed for each game.

The joystick function is activated by little sets of spring contacts inside the unit. As it's moved in different directions, you'll hear tiny clicking sounds that indicate that contact was properly made. After several weeks of hard use, upward movements of the joystick stopped working. When I opened it up, I found one of the springs had popped out of place. Two minutes with a screwdriver and needle-nosed pliers, however, put it right. I wish all joysticks were as easy to repair.

Using the Ultimate Superstick is a pleasure. It's one of the most functional, playable joysticks available.

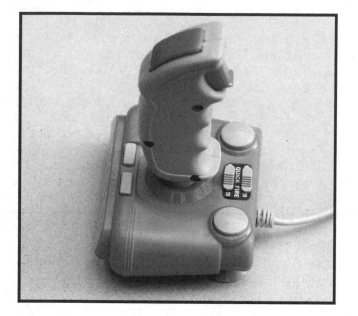

Name	The Zinger
Price	$15.99

Ratings

Construction	6
Features	7
Responsiveness	10
Play Value	7.67

Review

The Zinger is a pistol-grip joystick with 360-degree motion control. The grip is fashioned like a handlebar grip on a bicycle and has firing buttons (B) on both the top and front. You can use either your index finger or thumb to shoot. There are two A buttons—one on each side and to the front of the grip, so the Zinger can be used by right- or left-handed players. Each button has its own single-position turbo mode switch.

The unit comes with a 9-foot cord and has stress relief at its base to keep the cord from becoming frayed. The con-

219

nector fits snugly into the NES; so snugly, in fact, that it's difficult to insert and remove. At least you won't have to worry about it falling out. The Zinger doesn't appear to be as sturdy as some of the other units tested. Not that it will fall apart during use. It just doesn't feel as good.

The Zinger is very responsive, yet unsuitable for many NES games. The oversized grip makes it top heavy and difficult to control for fast-action games or those that require small movements. Four suction cups secure it in place. Vigorous movements, however, tend to unstick the suction cups. You'll find the Zinger most useful in games where character motion is somewhat limited. Bump 'n' Jump is a good example. Logically, driving and flying games seem most appropriate.

At $15.99 retail, it's the least expensive controller with separate A and B rapid-fire switches. Still, for another dollar you could pick up Beeshu's Zipper instead—my preferred low-cost controller. Although the Zipper doesn't have 360-degree control, it is usable for every game.

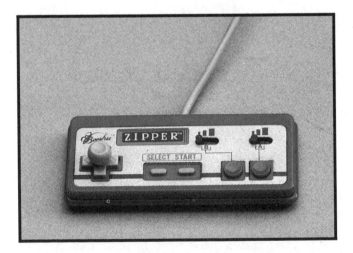

Name   The Zipper
Price $16.99

Ratings
Construction  8
Features 6
Responsiveness 9
Play Value   7.67

Review

The Zipper is a favorite of mine. It's the same size and shape as the original NES controller, but has an extra-long cord and separate, three-position A and B rapid-fire switches. It also includes a stubby (about ½-inch high) joystick piece that can be inserted into the control pad to give you the feel of a joystick. With a few games—particularly those that only allow movements along the X/Y axes, you may prefer using it without the joystick attachment.

The Zipper is made of plastic and is held together by several tiny screws. Although you can disassemble the unit, there's nothing inside that you can repair—unless you're on a first-name basis with a soldering iron. They'll take a lot of abuse, but, like the original NES controllers they were designed to replace, will begin to lose some responsiveness over time. After five weeks of heavy use, the A button began to fade on me. But at $16.99, you can easily afford to replace it.

The Zipper comes in five colors, so if you buy two different ones, you'll never have to untangle the cords to see which one belongs to each player. The Zipper is a good choice if you're looking for an inexpensive controller with rapid-fire capabilities.

Camerica Corporation

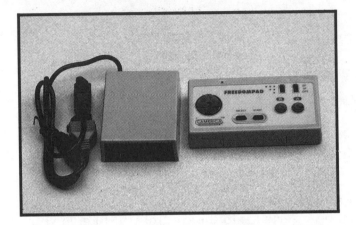

Name	Freedom Pad
Price	$39.99

Ratings

Construction	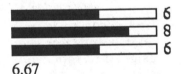	6
Features		8
Responsiveness		6
Play Value	6.67	

Review

The Freedom Pad is a hand-held remote control unit that looks a lot like the standard NES controller. It's about an inch thick so it can contain the necessary electronic parts and batteries. Its shape makes it very comfortable to hold. The remote sensor comes with a cord that's slightly longer than normal. This allows the sensor point forward, since the cord doesn't drag it out of position.

You can set rapid-fire to any of three levels. Both A and B buttons, however, are controlled by a single switch, making the feature unusable in games where A is used for jumping. You can also select whether the Freedom Pad will operate in one- or two-player mode. In games where two players take turns, the unit can be passed between them after flipping a switch. In two-players simultaneous games, you'll need two Freedom Pad controllers.

I had two problems while testing the unit. First, there were occasional misfires on the different buttons. Second, and considerably more serious, the player select button failed after only a short time and I was unable to repair it. I could only set it for player 2. Like most controllers, the unit does come with a 90-day warranty, so it can be repaired if you have similar problems. On the basis of the performance of the unit I tested, however, I cannot recommend the Freedom Pad.

Note: Although not licensed by Nintendo, Camerica produces controllers that are compatible with the NES.

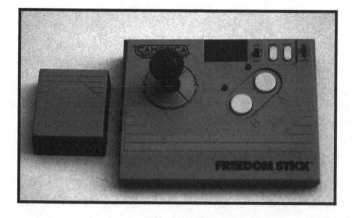

Name   Freedom Stick
Price $69.99

Ratings
Construction   9
Features   9
Responsiveness   10
Play Value   9.33

Review

The Freedom Stick has the same feature list as Supersonic the Joystick, but minus the double set of A and B buttons. It is a remote unit with rapid fire, one- and two-player capability, and 360-degree joystick control.

The remote sensor connects to the NES through a short adapter plug that keeps it even with the playing area. If you have other systems, you'll find that the Freedom Stick can do double- or even triple-duty. A second connector is provided that allows it to be used with the Sega Master System; the Atari 2600, 7800, and XE Game System; the Commodore 64 and 128 computers; and the Commodore Vic 20.

The heavy-duty joystick is stiffer than those on the other units tested. Small children may have difficulty with it, but it's fine for older children, teens, and adults. (If you've used a self-centering joystick with a computer before, you'll probably feel at home with the Freedom Stick.)

The Freedom Stick also shares the same shortcomings as Supersonic the Joystick. It is expensive (part of the expense is for an additional adapter you may or may not need), the suction cups frequently pop out (this sounds like a job for Super Glue), and rapid-fire cannot be set individually for the A and B buttons. Of course, you can flip rapid-fire on and off at will, but it's more convenient for many games to just leave B on and A off.

Still, if you have the cash, you'll find the Freedom Stick a very serviceable unit. It responds accurately, it's well built, and the joystick has a solid, positive feel to it.

Note: Although not licensed by Nintendo, Camerica produces controllers that are compatible with the NES.

Name	Supersonic the Joystick
Price	$59.99

Ratings

Construction		9
Features		9
Responsiveness		9
Play Value	9.00	

Review

Supersonic the Joystick is a remote control unit with a sleek, hi-tech design. It's triangle-shaped with a front edge that's about 1½ times higher than the trailing edge. The 360-degree joystick is center-mounted, and two sets of oversized A and B buttons are positioned to either side of it. Smaller round Start and Select buttons are set in the center rear of the unit.

Like most good remote controllers, this one has a power on/off switch to help conserve the batteries. It can be set for one- or two-player games with the same switch. Other switches are for rapid-fire (it's either on or off for both buttons at once) and for left- or right-handed play. Depending on this last setting, either the left-hand or right-hand A and B buttons will be active. Whenever a button of any type is pressed, a string of LEDs above the joystick flashes in sequence.

Supersonic the Joystick has three suction cups that can be used to hold it down, but—like so many of the units—

225

they don't stick well and sometimes pop out of the base. The remote sensor is intelligently designed. It avoids the use of connecting cords altogether by plugging straight into the two controller outlets. Unlike other remote sensors, there's no need to worry about it suddenly sliding around and facing the wrong direction.

Among tabletop remote units, Supersonic the Joystick is definitely among the better ones. It's attractive and very responsive. The only drawbacks are the relatively high retail price and the inability to separately set rapid-fire for each button.

Note: Although not licensed by Nintendo, Camerica produces controllers that are compatible with the NES.

Nintendo of America, Inc.

Name	NES Advantage
Price	$39.95

Ratings

Construction	▬▬▬▬▬▬□	9
Features	▬▬▬▬▬▬□	9
Responsiveness	▬▬▬▬▬▬▬	10
Play Value	9.33	

Review

The NES Advantage, partly because it's made by Nintendo and partly because of its exceptional feature list, has set the standard for high-quality NES controllers. It's made of heavy-duty plastic. Everything about it says sturdy. Because of it's weighted base, it also happens to be one of the heaviest controllers around. While the added weight makes it impractical to hold it in your hand, it does help keep the controller firmly in place when resting on the floor or table.

Features for the Advantage include individual speed adjustment knobs for A and B turbo mode, slow motion, and a switch for selecting one- or two-player games (both players can use the Advantage by moving it back and forth between them on their turn). You can quickly move in or out of turbo mode by clicking either of the small buttons above the oversized A and B buttons. The joystick is on the left side of the unit, and the A and B buttons are in center right.

The NES Advantage has a stylish high-tech design, making it look—as well as work—like the classy unit it is. Perhaps the only flaw in its construction, however, is related to this design. The front is beveled, tapering off to a forward edge about half the unit's thickness. With my adult hands, this led to frequent cramps because of the uncomfortable position my hand was forced into.

Overall, I like the Advantage. The choice of features is excellent, the unit is sturdy, and it's extremely responsive. (I can't remember ever getting mad because I hit a button but the character didn't jump.) Because of the design, however, I suggest play-testing it at a friend's house for at least a two-hour stretch before committing to one.

Name	NES Max
Price	$19.95

Ratings

Construction		9
Features		7
Responsiveness		7
Play Value	7.66	

Review

Although about the same size and weight as the standard NES controller, the Max has an unusual shape—something like a wing or an inverted letter U. It includes two sets of A and B buttons. The top ones are the standard buttons and the two tiny ones beneath are for turbo or rapid-fire mode. Rather than grappling with switches to change modes, all you have to do is press a different button.

The Max's other feature is a unique *thumb-wheel* that provides 360-degree control, much like a joystick or trackball. If you're used to a trackball, however, you may find it hard to adjust to the thumb-wheel. Operating a thumb-wheel isn't just a matter of pushing or rotating in the right direction. You also have to press down at the same time. I found it difficult to remember to do this (it wasn't natural), so many of my movements had no onscreen effect.

There's a small circle that surrounds the thumb-wheel. If you press there, it works just like a joystick. In general, to avoid having to think about whether I was using the thumb-wheel correctly, I used the surrounding circle instead.

My feeling is that if you can adjust to and like the thumb-wheel, the Max is a good, inexpensive choice for a controller replacement. If not, there are others in this price range that may suit you better.

Feature Comparison Chart

Company	Controller Name	Retail Price	Cord Length	Remote Control	360 Deg. Control	Rapid Fire	Slow Motion	Left/Rt. Buttons	Suction Cups	2-Player Mode
Acclaim Entertainment	Wireless Infrared Remote	$39.95	—	√		√				
Bandai America	Hyper	$29.99	7.5 ft.			√				
	Hyper Stick	$34.99	7.5 ft.		√	√				
	Mega Controller	$42.99	7.5 ft.		√	√	√			
	Super Controller	$7.99	—			√				
Beeshu	Jazz Stick	$22.99	4 ft.		√	√			√	
	Ultimate Superstick	$39.99	9 ft.		√	√	√	√	√	
	Zinger	$15.99	9 ft.		√	√		√	√	
	Zipper	$16.99	9 ft.			√				
	Zoomer	$22.99	10 ft.			√	√		√	
Broderbund Software	U-Force	$69.95	4 - 6 ft.		√	√				
Camerica Corporation	Freedom Pad	$39.99	—	√		√				√
	Freedom Stick	$69.99	—	√	√	√				√
	Supersonic the Joystick	$59.99	—	√	√	√		√	√	√
LJN Toys	Roll & Rocker	$40.00	7 ft.			√				
Mattell Toys	Power Glove	$80.00	Unknown		√	√	√			
Nintendo of America	NES Advantage	$39.95	7.5 ft.		√	√	√	·		√
	NES Max	$19.95	8 ft.		√	√				

Note: Although not licensed by Nintendo, Camerica manufactures controllers that are compatible with the NES.

Special-Purpose Contollers

Power Glove

Manufacturer	Mattell Toys
Price	$80.00

Ratings
Construction	Not Rated
Features	Not Rated
Responsiveness	Not Rated
Play Value	Not Rated

The Power Glove was not available for review at the time
this book was written, so no ratings are provided. The information below is based on press releases and discussions
with the manufacturer.

Review

If you want to get closer to your controller and the NES games you play, Mattell intends to release you can wear! The Power Glove (available in two sizes) fits over your hand and forearm. The actions of the player's hand dictate the actions of the characters and objects in the game. An *L-bar* (L-shaped sensor bar) is placed on top of the TV and receives the motion signals transmitted by the glove.

The face of the glove contains the standard A, B, Select, and Start buttons, and provides both turbo and slow-motion modes. A programmable keypad with the ten digits and Enter and Clear buttons lets you customize the glove's motion-detecting responses for each game. Essentially, the player teaches the glove the hand motions that will replace the normal joystick motions. In Rad Racer, for example, the player uses the glove to hold an imaginary steering wheel, and turns it in space to make the onscreen car turn. Braking is performed by simply pushing downward with the glove—like pressing a car's brake pedal.

According to Mattell, the Power Glove is compatible with all joystick-controlled games. The Owner's Manual will contain illustrated instructions for configuring 30 popular Nintendo titles for play with the unit.

The Power Glove is scheduled to be released in Fall 1989. *Several games (Super Glove Ball, Glove Pilot, and the Terror of "Tech Town") are being developed specifically for the Power Glove and should be available at about the same time.*

Roll & Rocker

Manufacturer	LJN Toys, Inc.
Price	$40.00

Ratings

Construction	██████████████	10
Features	████████☐	6
Responsiveness	██████████████	10
Play Value	8.67	

Review

Picture a turtle flipped on its back. Now try and stand on the turtle's stomach without falling off (or annoying it). This will give you some idea of what the Roll & Rocker is all about.

The Roll & Rocker replaces the standard controller's control pad, handling all directional movements. There's a joystick port in the front of the unit that is used to hook in a standard controller so you can use its buttons (A, B, Start, and Select).

Using the Roll & Rocker is a matter of rocking in the direction you want your character to move—up, down, right, left, or diagonally. Its intent —and it succeeds well at this—is to bring new life to some of your old games. Picture playing a surfing or skateboarding game with the Roll & Rocker, for instance. Now there's a way to really get into your games, much more than with a standard controller. Your body motions dictate onscreen movement.

The games that the unit works best with are those that don't require fine control of movement or lots of little movements. Playing Super Mario Bros., for example, is very difficult. Also, I wouldn't recommend it for people with weak ankles. If you're concerned that you or your kids are wasting away in front of the tube, the Roll & Rocker will get them on their feet again and give them a little exercise in the process.

U-Force

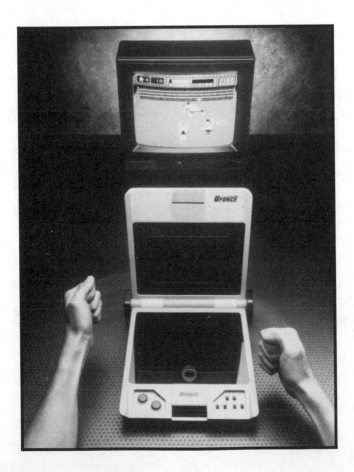

Manufacturer	Broderbund Software
Price	$69.95

Ratings

Construction	Not Rated
Features	Not Rated
Responsiveness	Not Rated
Play Value	Not Rated

The U-Force was not available for review at the time this book was written, so no ratings are provided. The information below is based on press releases and discussions with the manufacturer.

Review

The U-Force employs a new concept in NES controllers. Instead of pushing buttons and moving a joystick or control pad, the U-Force allows you to control game play by sensing the movements of your hands in free space. As your hands pass in front of one or more motion sensors, your actions are translated directly into game commands. To punch, for example, actually punch at the controller, rather than pressing a button. To steer a car, pretend to hold a steering wheel and steer normally.

The U-Force connects to the NES through a standard cable, and requires no batteries or separate power supply. It has ten motion sensors scattered over its surface (see U-Force Console Diagram). Sensors 1 through 8 are used to control movement, speed, direction, and firing, assuming the game you're playing offers these options. The Select and Start buttons are used as they normally are. On some games, Select and/or Start actions can also be controlled by hand gestures. The sensor labelled *Top*, for example, can sometimes be used in place of the Start button.

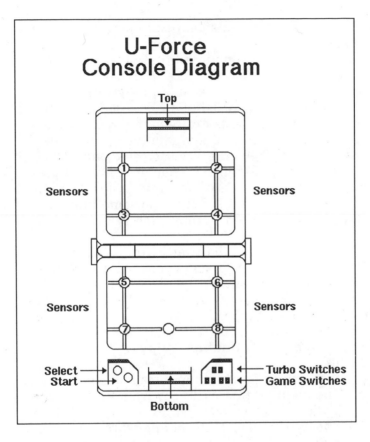

U-Force
Console Diagram

Top

Sensors

Sensors

Sensors

Sensors

Select

Start

Turbo Switches

Game Switches

Bottom

Two switches are used to set turbo mode or rapid-fire. Once switched on, they function the same way as on a standard controller that has this feature. There appears to be no way, however, to set the turbo rate.

To use U-Force with most games, it's necessary to do two things. First, the unit must be positioned correctly. There are three possible playing positions: laid flat, upright (with the two halves at a 90-degree angle to each other), or upright with a slight tilt. Second, the four game switches (lower right-hand corner of the diagram) must be set. There are six usable switch combinations, including one reserved

for games that will be created specifically for play on the
U-Force.

Several accessories are included that players will find
helpful while learning to use U-Force. A T-bar handle with
firing grips can be inserted into a hole in the unit (the
empty circle above the sensor labelled *Bottom* in the diagram). When the T-bar or grips are held, your hands are
placed in the proper position to activate the appropriate
motion sensors. *(Note: There are no electronic parts in
either the T-bar or the firing grips. They are for hand positioning only, and are not required for any game.)* The other
accessory is a Power Bar that fits into the same hole. Its
purpose is to extend the field of play slightly to each side
of the unit.

What games can U-Force be used with? According to
the manual, almost any game except those that require the
NES Zapper or Power Pad should be playable. Specific instructions for configuring six games (Mike Tyson's Punch-
Out!!, Top Gun, Rad Racer, Excitebike, Super Mario Bros.,
and Kung Fu) are included. Game switch settings and a
recommended U-Force positioning setup are offered for another 60 games.

Is it easier to use or harder than a standard controller?
According to the manual, this will vary from game to game.
It's something you'll have to get used to.

*Note: To encourage other NES manufacturers to write
games specifically for the U-Force, Broderbund has created
a software developer's support group. U-Force is scheduled
for release in Fall 1989.*

The Zoomer

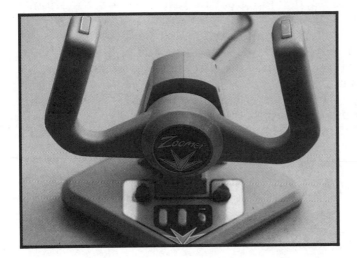

Manufacturer   Beeshu, Inc.
Price $22.99

Ratings
Construction   ████████████ 10
Features   ████████▢ 7
Responsiveness   ██████████▢ 9
Play Value   8.67

Review

Games where driving or flying are done from the player's perspective often seem to be missing something. Face it. It's hard to feel like you're driving a a car or flying a plane when all you have for steering is a tiny control pad.

Beeshu felt you deserved something better, so it created the Zoomer. The Zoomer is designed to look and act like a pilot's yoke or steering wheel. You can pull back on it or push it forward, and steer right, left, or diagonally. The buttons are mounted on the tips of the handles, adding to the realism when machine gunfire is needed. The

☐ Special-Purpose Controllers

Zoomer is so close to the real thing that players who use it can't seem to help making "vroom-vroom" noises.

Beeshu included some great features like slow motion, separate A and B button rapid-fire controls, and a ten-foot–long cord. The Zoomer is best used when firmly mounted to a playing surface, such as a table. (Its own box will do in a pinch.) Super powerful suction cups on the base do the job nicely.

Although other types of NES games can be played with a Zoomer, you'll probably want to switch back to a standard controller. But for the right type of game, the Zoomer is an excellent, inexpensive addition to any controller collection.

Controller Play Value Ratings

Controller	Rating
Freedom Pad	6.67
Freedom Stick	9.33
Hyper	7.67
Hyper Stick	9
Jazz Stick	8.33
Mega Controller	9.33
NES Advantage	9.33
NES Max	7.67
Roll & Rocker	8.67
Super Controller	7.67
Supersonic the Joystick	9
Ultimate SuperStick	9
Wireless Infrared Remote Cont.	8.67
Zinger	7.67
Zipper	7.67
Zoomer	8.67

Other Accessories

Every time there's a new craze, the manufacturer usually cashes in on it with a host of items featuring the best-known characters. Posters, lunch boxes, T-shirts, and the like frequently make the rounds for about six months and then end up somewhere on the sales racks.

Other than a few T-shirts, you'd be hard-pressed to find any Nintendo paraphernalia out there. Just so you don't feel lost without having something else to spend your money on, here are two of my favorites.

Super Mario Bros. Trophy

| **Manufacturer** | Hasbro, Inc. |
| **Retail Price** | $1.99 |

As a gift for your own Nintendo hero, this one can't be beat! It's a trophy featuring one of six different Super Mario Bros. action scenes (Mario hurls a fireball, Mario stomps the Goombas, Mario kicks one of the Hammer Brothers, Bowser guards Princess Toadstool, Mario runs from Bullet Bill, and a Blooper chases Mario). Each trophy stands a little over four inches high and is mounted on a sturdy plastic base. The painted characters are also made of durable plastic.

On the base of the trophy is a sticker where you can enter the game player's name, high score, and the date it was achieved. (In case he or she improves, the trophy also comes with a spare sticker you can paste over the original one.) The trophies are well made, inexpensive, and look good. Just the thing for your trophy case.

Nintendo Cereal System

Classification	Miscellaneous
Players	As many as you have bowls
Controller	Standard spoon
Pause	If you feel like it
Restart at Last Level	No, but you wouldn't want to
Manufacturer	Ralston Purina Company
Retail Price	$2.79 (approx.)

Ratings

Instructions	4
Features	10
Graphics	4
Sound	6
Challenge	5
Play Value	6.05

Review
First, there was the NES. Now try the NCS—the Nintendo Cereal System! *It kind of makes you wonder what will be next . . . Teenage Mutant Ninja Bran Flakes?*

Instructions
No manual is included, but then you probably know how this one works. Check the side panel for some special game tips you won't find anywhere else.

Features
NCS borrows a packaging concept that has had success in the candy world. Inside the box are two bags of cereal: Mario on one side and Zelda on the other. The two cereals are described as "Fruity" and "Berry." Sounds like a good name for a Saturday morning cartoon team. They're further described as having "two different natural and artificial flavors." In case you're interested, Super Mario Bros. is the one with the natural flavors—although it doesn't mention specifically where in nature the flavors come from.

241

The current version of the NCS includes an innovative and appropriate prize: a miniature Zelda or Mario pinball game. For safety's sake (and in case you crave more sugar), you can eat the balls it uses. They're made out of candy.

Sound and Graphics

The graphics in the two sections of the NCS are the reverse of their game counterparts. Where the original Zelda graphics were far from state of the art, those in the cereal—for the most part—are easily recognizable. *The hearts and boomerangs are my favorites.* On the other hand, although the Super Mario Bros. game has some of the best graphics around, it suffers in its cereal version. The yellow things are 1-UP mushrooms and Goombas, I think.

I don't get it. No snap, crackle, or pop. In fact, unless you whack them with your spoon, the NCS just floats there. Unlike the inferior Brand X cereals, however, the NCS *does* stay crunchy in milk. You'll have to make the sound effects yourself. (And I was so hoping for a cereal with a theme song.)

Challenge

It's easy to work your way through either the Zelda or Super Mario Bros. portions of the NCS. I don't suggest that you try it in one session, however.

As a parent, one of my biggest challenges was to get the kids to brush their teeth afterwards. Since sugar is second on the list of ingredients and the manufacturer neglects to mention the number of grams in an average serving, I'd consider this one of your challenges, too.

Play Value

Even if it is a cute idea and has a neat prize, it's hard to recommend the NCS. I don't think kids should be encouraged to play with their food.

Tips, Tricks, and Strategies

■ Unless your town has fluoridated water, keep the serving size to the recommended single ounce.
■ To avoid unnecessary confusion, never try to eat both versions at the same time.

A Parent's Guide to Nintendo

Optimizing Play on a Limited Budget

Although the initial cost of a basic Nintendo set is only about $100, add in a few hot new game titles and a souped-up controller or two, and it's easy to double or triple your initial investment. If you haven't convinced your kids yet that you aren't made of money, here are a few suggestions for keeping costs down while maximizing the play value your children get from the NES.

Nintendo Clubs

School-age children don't need to invest a fortune to experience a variety of Nintendo games. Either formally or informally, kids can start a Nintendo club, for example. Although $30 to $50 is a lot of money for a game—particularly for one ten-year-old, it's easily managed by a group of kids.

By assessing monthly dues of a few dollars, a group can decide on and purchase a new game each month or so. On a rotating basis, each group member might use the cartridge for a specific number of days before passing it to the next member. In this way, each child can play at least a dozen new cartridges each year for the price of a single game. Similarly, games that members already own can be temporarily traded with the others.

Club membership also helps foster a sense of belonging, serves a social function (common topics of conversation, sharing game tips, and so on), and encourages friendly competition.

The Nintendo Allowance

If a club isn't to your child's liking—not everyone is a join-er—or it isn't practical because of the distance between children, nothing prevents you as a parent from giving your child an allowance *paid in Nintendo games and controllers, rather than dollars.* Establish a list of chores that your child is expected to perform. If faithfully carried out, he or she can be rewarded with a new cartridge every four to eight weeks—one that you select together.

The concepts of *cost* and *money* often mean little to a young child. If payment is given in terms that the child can understand and appreciate (a new game, for instance), it can help teach these concepts. This arrangement demonstrates that a specific amount and quality of work can be exchanged for a game of a specific cost. Of course, you can also give a standard allowance and encourage your child to save his money for games—reinforcing the concept of saving and making it more the child's responsibility.

Rent vs. Buy

Games you want for the long run are obvious "buy" candidates. What about the hundred or so games that you or your child aren't sure about? No matter what you read about a cartridge there's no substitute for hands-on experience when it comes to choosing games. In the last year or so, NES games have begun showing up at the movie rental shops. For a dollar or two a night, you can try out almost any game, often shortly after it has been released.

Getting Things Under Control

Make no mistake about it. When magazines describe Nintendo games as additive, they aren't kidding. Several years ago, we saw the same phenomenon in video arcades. Many kids spent all their free time and money in the local arcades. Now with the convenience of the NES, kids can get just as involved in game play without leaving the comfort of their homes—in some cases to the detriment of grades and to the exclusion of other activities.

The difference between controlling NES play and letting it control you often comes down to a matter of emphasis. If your children see Nintendo play as their right, you've already lost the battle. Punish them by taking away something that they consider a right, and you become the ogre.

If behavioral psychologists are correct (and I agree with them on this), the best way to encourage positive behavior in children is to provide a suitable reward or reinforcement. Establish Nintendo play as a reward rather than a right. If your child finishes his homework or puts in an hour of piano practice, he can play the Nintendo for a designated amount of time. He does something good, you do something good. If it's viewed as a fair exchange, everyone stays happy.

On those occasions when your child doesn't live up to his part of the bargain (nobody's perfect), you should be able to withhold NES play without it being viewed as a punishment. Instead, you can explain it in terms of breach of contract. If you hired a handyman to paint your house and he never showed up, you wouldn't pay him. Similarly, if your child doesn't do what he agreed to do, you can't be expected to reward his behavior.

Lessons in Living

There are some valuable lessons that can be learned from Nintendo game play. Sharing and taking turns are easily taught if you have more than one child or if they play with friends. Competition will naturally occur and, if it's not forced or heavily stressed, can be a positive thing for children.

Equally important is showing how beneficial cooperative play can be. Many games now include a two-player simultaneous mode. In Bubble Bobble, for example, children quickly see that they can advance through the levels faster if they help each other.

And you thought they were just playing games . . .

NES Games and Violence

With the exception of a handful of educational and party games, many NES games involve some degree of violence. To complete a game, it's not unusual to destroy hundreds or thousands of animals, monsters, or people. Even some sports games toss in a gratuitous fist fight or two for added "realism." At the low end of the spectrum, we have violence against make-believe creatures, often using magic weapons. The most violent games feature direct violence against humans with a variety of real weapons. Frequently all that's missing is the blood.

To its credit, Nintendo has instructed its licensees (the game publishers) not to use words like *kill* in the games and instruction manuals. Instead, they opt for softer terms such as *destroy* or *defeat*. Language aside, death and killing are implicit in many games.

Does this sound familiar? After playing several games, my five-year-old son began talking almost incessantly about killing things. From the few games he had played, he immediately generalized to all others. That is, to win a game, you have to kill things. It so colored his thinking that it took over 15 minutes to explain to him that the goal of Donkey Kong was merely to run a series of mazes; that you cannot hit, shoot, or kill the giant gorilla—nor would you want to.

The Positive Side to NES Violence

We're all exposed to violence in our lives. It would be naive to think that we can shelter our children from it. Forbid your kids to play with guns, and sooner or later they'll improvise with sticks or their fingers. Violence is an established element in Nintendo games, so we all have to decide how we'll deal with it.

Because they are games, violence is usually depicted as a black-and-white matter. "I am the good guy and they (the monsters, enemy pilots, or gang members) are the bad guys. It's okay to destroy them and bad for me to get hurt." Life, unfortunately, isn't so simple. It's a matter of perspective. How many of the bad guys in your life actually thought that they were the bad guys?

Even with their simple-minded approach to violence, NES games can provide excellent material for family discussions. All children can relate to being hurt. While playing 1943, my five-year-old started to think about the people in the planes he was shooting at. He wondered what they were feeling. Was that what war is like?

Getting Involved

I am not a proponent of censorship. Nor do I advocate any system that would restrict the sale or marketing of games. What I do suggest is that parents get involved with young children's NES activities and take a good look at the games they play.

If you feel that limiting your child's exposure to violence is important, you may find the following material useful. To help identify suitable cartridges for your youngest children (ages 5 to 9), games have been rated for level of violence. Each game reviewed in this book is rated according to violent content and theme as either high, moderate, or low. The classifications are as follows:

High. The focus of the game is direct violence against humans. Killing is the object.

Moderate. The theme is violence, but against make-believe creatures; or there is violence against humans, but defeating them rather than killing is the object; or there is violence against humans, but it is incidental to the game or implied, rather than the game's focus.

Low. The game is nonviolent; or the emphasis is on defeating make-believe creatures rather than killing them. Weapons are frequently imaginary (magic powers, for example).

The violence ratings are not precise, and they only represent my opinions. They are intended to serve as rough guidelines (if you're looking for such guidelines), and are best used as a starting point for developing your own opinions on the matter. Violence ratings and brief comments about each game are presented at the end of this chapter.

Let me make something clear. Violence in games is not a novel concept, nor was it invented by NES. Violence has been in computer games for years. The NES industry—with the constant influx of new manufacturers—now appears to be ready to move on to the next major plateau in game design.

A Call for Better Games

There's little reason we can't expect more imaginative plot lines; ones that don't stress violence or a kill-or-be-killed attitude. It's easy to create another violent game: kill a lot of things, reward the player with power and hit points as he does, and work up to the final confrontation with the evil lord of the monsters. It's difficult, on the other hand, to come up with an imaginative, nonviolent adventure that rewards problem-solving skills and is still fun to play.

The portrayal of women in games could stand some work. Other than the heroine Athena and the Princess in Super Mario Bros. 2, women are usually depicted as kidnap victims. The only nonvictims that come to mind are the whip-wielding Lindas (Double Dragon) and Pretty Amy (Lee Trevino's Fighting Golf). It's nice to see some females in NES games, but I don't think it's necessary to make them gang members or add *Pretty* as part of their names.

I'd also like to see a greater emphasis on the Nintendo's potential for early education and more games written specifically for young children. The Nintendo is a good tool for developing eye/hand coordination and problem-solving skills. To be really useful for young children, however, games have to be created that require only elementary reading abilities, and simpler rules and controls. The Sesame Street games from Hi Tech Expressions are a good start toward this goal. More cartridges of this type will undoubtedly appear as additional manufacturers move to fill this market gap.

Violence Ratings

Games with High Violence

Bionic Commando
Shoot the enemy soldiers in face-to-face combat.

Double Dragon
Kill your human enemies with lethal karate moves, knives, whips, baseball bats, and anything else that's handy.

Golgo 13
Secret Agent Duke Togo uses his machine gun and sniper rifle to blow away the bad guys in a variety of realistic sequences.

Metal Gear
Use your military weapons (guns, grenades, and rocket launcher) to kill the enemy soldiers.

Operation Wolf
Shoot or blow up the bad guys and rescue the hostages.

P.O.W.
Use karate, knives, guns, and grenades to fight your way out of a P.O.W. camp.

Games with Moderate Violence

1943

Fighting against planes and ships. Violence against humans is only implied, not shown.

Athena

Lots of fighting using lots of weapons, but all directed against imaginary, animal-like creatures.

Blades of Steel

Contains gratuitous violence (fist-fights between players). Just like the real thing.

Blaster Master

Destroy the robots and alien creatures with a laser tank and other weapons. No humans other than the main character.

Castlevania II: Simon's Quest

Destroy all the monsters with your whip, daggers, and holy water.

Clash at Demonhead

Use your arsenal of weapons and super powers to blow away the evil little monsters of this land. Includes some human bosses, but they are few and far between.

Guerilla War

Lead the guerilla fighter to victory and rescue the hostages. Kill everyone with your machine gun, tank, bombs, and flamethrower. Although this probably should have a High Violence rating, the cartoonish look of the tiny characters tempers the violence somewhat.

Jackal

Use your powerful all-terrain jeep and its guns to rescue hostages from the enemy. Like Guerilla War (above), the enemy soldiers are so small that the violence isn't quite so blatant.

Karnov

Karnov, the fire-breathing circus strongman, must use his super power, cunning, and weapons to destroy all the unusual creatures. Although a few are humanlike, the majority are clearly imaginary.

The Legend of Zelda

Brave little Link must avoid or destroy a variety of make-believe creatures with his magic sword, bombs, and flame.

Legendary Wings

The god Ares has given you wings and weapons to combat the forces of evil. Destroy the imaginary creatures and monsters before they destroy you. Shooting arcade game.

Mega Man II

Help the super robot Mega Man defeat Dr. Wiley's evil robots with his gun and secret powers.

Mickey Mousecapade

Mickey and Minnie use magic throwing stars to try to defeat the creatures that block their way. A few, like Pete the pirate, use real weapons (knives, for example).

RoboWarrior

RoboWarrior must battle the aliens and evil lords on a distant space colony.

Super Mario Bros. 2

Only a little nastier than the original Super Mario Bros. The enemies are still weird creatures, but Mario's weapons arsenal now includes bombs.

Stealth ATF

Pilot your fighter plane in pursuit of enemy fighters. Only the planes are shown.

Teenage Mutant Ninja Turtles

Using a variety of Ninja weapons (Bo, Katana, Nunchuku, Sai, and Shuriken), help the turtles destroy Shredder and his evil companions. Loads of violence, but directed against imaginary creatures rather than people.

Tiger-Heli

Blow up houses, tanks, planes, and war ships. Violence against humans is implied, but not shown.

Zelda II: The Adventure of Link

Destroy the imaginary denizens of Link's world using a sword and magic powers.

Games with Low Violence

Adventures of Lolo

Strategy game. Player must use his or her wits to win, rather than strength or force.

Anticipation

Nonviolent party game.

Bubble Bobble

Defeat Baron von Blubba's creatures by trapping them in bubbles and changing them into bonus prizes like candy.

Bump 'n' Jump

Use your little roadster to bump the bad guys' cars off the road. Just cars; no people.

California Games
Skateboarding, BMX riding, surfing, foot bag, and Frisbee contests in the warm California sun.

City Connection
Paint the highways of the world with your little car while evading the police. Throw oil barrels at the police to make them spin out of your way.

Gotcha!
Shoot members of the opposing team in this game of Capture the Flag. The twist, however, is that you use a gun that shoots paint instead of bullets. Mark them with paint and they're out of the game.

Hoops
Nonviolent street basketball game. Players occasionally fall down from the usual charging and pushing fouls.

Kid Kool
Avoid, jump on, or throw Wickey at the unusual creatures that populate this strange land. Defeating the creatures, rather than destroying them, is the emphasis.

Lee Trevino's Fighting Golf
The only thing that's violent about the game is its name. (Maybe you were expecting punch-out sequences over who won the last hole between guys wearing funny pants? Dumb name.)

Mappy-Land
Nonviolent arcade game for kids. Find presents for the mouse's girlfriend while trying to outrun and outwit his pursuers.

Marble Madness
Race a marble through several 3-D mazes while trying to avoid the bizarre creatures that live there.

Othello

Popular board game (based on the ancient game of Go) converted for play on the NES. No violence.

Pac-Man

Use your arcade skills to avoid or catch ghosts while clearing mazes of dots.

R.C. Pro-AM

Race radio-controlled cars around the track. Weapons can be used to temporarily knock other cars out of the race.

Sesame Street 1 2 3

Learn elementary math and shape-recognition skills with Ernie and Grover.

Super Mario Bros.

Defeat the creatures of the kingdom and rescue the princess.

Taboo the Sixth Sense

Fortune-telling game. No violence.

Tetris

Computerized puzzle. No violence.

The Three Stooges

Violence is deemphasized. Contains one Stooges slap-fight sequence strictly for laughs.

Game Index (by Classification)

Controller Index